Great Military Commanders
Dwight D. Eisenhower
A Biography

Compiled by
Yohan Trevino

Scribbles

Year of Publication 2018

ISBN : 9789352979424

Book Published by

Scribbles

(An Imprint of Alpha Editions)

email - alphaedis@gmail.com

Produced by: PediaPress GmbH
Limburg an der Lahn
Germany
http://pediapress.com/

The content within this book was generated collaboratively by volunteers. Please be advised that nothing found here has necessarily been reviewed by people with the expertise required to provide you with complete, accurate or reliable information. Some information in this book may be misleading or simply wrong. Alpha Editions and PediaPress does not guarantee the validity of the information found here. If you need specific advice (for example, medical, legal, financial, or risk management) please seek a professional who is licensed or knowledgeable in that area.

Sources, licenses and contributors of the articles and images are listed in the section entitled "References". Parts of the books may be licensed under the GNU Free Documentation License. A copy of this license is included in the section entitled "GNU Free Documentation License"

The views and characters expressed in the book are those of the contributors and his/her imagination and do not represent the views of the Publisher.

Contents

Articles   **1**

Eisenhower   **1**
    Dwight D. Eisenhower 1

Presidency   **69**
    Presidency of Dwight D. Eisenhower 69

Appendix   **119**
    References 119
    Article Sources and Contributors 126
    Image Sources, Licenses and Contributors 127

Article Licenses   **131**

Index   **133**

Eisenhower

Dwight D. Eisenhower

Dwight D. Eisenhower	

34th President of the United States	
In office January 20, 1953 – January 20, 1961	
Vice President	Richard Nixon
Preceded by	Harry S. Truman
Succeeded by	John F. Kennedy
1st Supreme Allied Commander Europe	
In office April 2, 1951 – May 30, 1952	
President	Harry S. Truman

Deputy	Arthur Tedder
Preceded by	position established
Succeeded by	Matthew Ridgway
16th Chief of Staff of the Army	
In office November 19, 1945 – February 6, 1948	
President	Harry S. Truman
Deputy	J. Lawton Collins
Preceded by	George Marshall
Succeeded by	Omar Bradley
Military Governor of the U.S. Occupation Zone in Germany	
In office May 8, 1945 – November 10, 1945	
President	Harry S. Truman
Preceded by	position established
Succeeded by	George S. Patton (acting) Joseph T. McNarney
13th President of Columbia University	
In office 1948–1953	
Preceded by	Frank D. Fackenthal
Succeeded by	Grayson L. Kirk
Personal details	
Born	David Dwight Eisenhower October 14, 1890 Denison, Texas, U.S.
Died	March 28, 1969 (aged 78) Washington, D.C., U.S.
Resting place	Dwight D. Eisenhower Presidential Library, Museum and Boyhood Home, Abilene, Kansas, U.S.
Political party	Republican
Spouse(s)	Mamie Geneva Doud (m. 1916)
Children	• Doud • John

Relatives	Ida Stover (Mother)
Education	United States Military Academy (BS)
Signature	*Dwight D Eisenhower*
Military service	
Allegiance	United States
Service/branch	United States Army
Years of service	1915–1953, 1961–1969
Rank	General of the Army
Battles/wars	• World War I • World War II
Awards	• Army Distinguished Service Medal (5) • Navy Distinguished Service Medal • Legion of Merit • World War I Victory Medal • World War II Victory Medal • *See more*
Eisenhower's voice Dwight D. Eisenhower's first Inaugural Address, January 20, 1953	

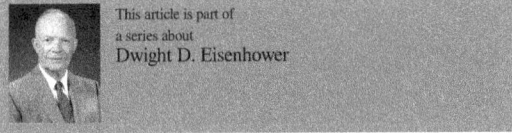

This article is part of a series about
Dwight D. Eisenhower

- Early Life
- Military Career

World War II

Supreme Allied Commander in Europe

- D-Day
- Operation Overlord

- Surrender of Germany
- VE-Day

- *Crusade in Europe*

President of the United States

- Presidency

First Term
- Draft movement
- 1952 Campaign
  - Election
- 1st Inauguration
- Korean War
- Atoms for Peace
- Cold War
  - New Look
  - Domino theory
- Interstate Highway System

Second Term
- 1956 campaign
  - Election
- 2nd Inauguration
- Eisenhower Doctrine
- Sputnik crisis
- Missile gap
- NDEA
- NASA
- DARPA
- Civil Rights Act of 1957
- Little Rock Nine
- U-2 incident
- Farewell Address

Post-Presidency
- Legacy
- Presidential library and museum
- Tributes and memorials

- v
- t
- e[1]

Dwight David "Ike" Eisenhower (/ˈaɪzənhaʊ.ər/ *EYE-zən-how-ər*; October 14, 1890 – March 28, 1969) was an American army general and statesman who served as the 34th President of the United States from 1953 to 1961. During World War II, he was a five-star general in the United States Army and served as Supreme Commander of the Allied Expeditionary Forces in Europe. He was responsible for planning and supervising the invasion of North Africa in Operation Torch in 1942–43 and the successful invasion of France and Germany in 1944–45 from the Western Front.

Born **David Dwight Eisenhower** in Denison, Texas, he was raised in Kansas in a large family of mostly Pennsylvania Dutch ancestry. His family had a strong religious background. His mother was born a Lutheran, married as a River Brethren, and later became a Jehovah's Witness. Even so, Eisenhower did not belong to any organized church until 1952. He cited constant relocation during his military career as one reason. He graduated from West Point in 1915 and later married Mamie Doud, with whom he had two sons. During World War I, he was denied a request to serve in Europe and instead commanded a unit that trained tank crews. Following the war, he served under various generals and was promoted to the rank of brigadier general in 1941. After the U.S. entered World War II, Eisenhower oversaw the successful invasions of North Africa and Sicily before supervising the invasions of France and Germany. After the war, Eisenhower served as Army Chief of Staff and then took on the uncomfortable role as president of Columbia University. In 1951–52, he served as the first Supreme Commander of NATO.

In 1952, Eisenhower entered the presidential race as a Republican to block the foreign policies of Senator Robert A. Taft. He won that election and the 1956 election in landslides, both times defeating Adlai Stevenson II. He became the first Republican-elected President since Herbert Hoover in 1928. Eisenhower's main goals in office were to contain the expansion of the Soviet Union and reduce federal deficits. In 1953, he threatened the use of nuclear weapons until China agreed to terms regarding POWs in the Korean War. An armistice ended the stalemated conflict. His New Look policy of nuclear deterrence prioritized inexpensive nuclear weapons while reducing funding for expensive Army divisions. He continued Harry S. Truman's policy of recognizing the Republic of China as the legitimate government of China, and he won congressional approval of the Formosa Resolution. His administration provided major aid to help the French fight off Vietnamese Communists in the First Indochina War. After the French left he gave strong financial support to the new state of South Vietnam. He supported local military coups against governments in Iran and Guatemala. During the Suez Crisis of 1956, Eisenhower condemned the Israeli, British and French invasion of Egypt, and he forced them to withdraw. He also condemned the Soviet invasion during the Hungarian Revolution of 1956 but took no action. During the Syrian Crisis of 1957 he approved a CIA-MI6 plan to stage fake border incidents as an excuse for an invasion by Syria's pro-Western neighbours. After the Soviet Union launched Sputnik in 1957, Eisenhower authorized the establishment of NASA, which led to the Space Race. He deployed 15,000 soldiers during the 1958 Lebanon crisis. Near the end of his term, his efforts to set up a summit meeting with the Soviets collapsed when a U.S. spy plane was shot down over Russia. He approved the Bay of Pigs invasion, which was left to his successor to carry out.[2]

On the domestic front, Eisenhower was a moderate conservative who continued New Deal agencies and expanded Social Security. He covertly opposed Joseph McCarthy and contributed to the end of McCarthyism by openly invoking executive privilege. Eisenhower signed the Civil Rights Act of 1957 and sent Army troops to enforce federal court orders that integrated schools in Little Rock, Arkansas. His largest program was the Interstate Highway System. He promoted the establishment of strong science education via the National Defense Education Act. Eisenhower's two terms saw widespread economic prosperity except for a minor recession in 1958. In his farewell address to the nation, Eisenhower expressed his concerns about the dangers of massive military spending, particularly deficit spending and government contracts to private military manufacturers. He was voted Gallup's most admired man twelve times and also achieved widespread popular esteem both in and out of office. Historical evaluations of his presidency place him among the upper tier of U.S. presidents.

Early life and education

The Eisenhauer (German for "iron hewer/miner") family migrated from Karlsbrunn in Nassau-Saarbrücken, to North America, first settling in York, Pennsylvania, in 1741, and in the 1880s moving to Kansas. Accounts vary as to how and when the German name Eisenhauer was anglicized to Eisenhower.

Figure 1: *The Eisenhower family home, Abilene, Kansas*

Eisenhower's Pennsylvania Dutch ancestors, who were primarily farmers, included Hans Nikolaus Eisenhauer of Karlsbrunn, who migrated to Lancaster, Pennsylvania, in 1741.

Hans's great-great-grandson, David Jacob Eisenhower (1863–1942), was Eisenhower's father and was a college-educated engineer, despite his own father Jacob's urging to stay on the family farm. Eisenhower's mother, Ida Elizabeth (Stover) Eisenhower, born in Virginia, of German Protestant ancestry, moved to Kansas from Virginia. She married David on September 23, 1885, in Lecompton, Kansas, on the campus of their alma mater, Lane University.

David owned a general store in Hope, Kansas, but the business failed due to economic conditions and the family became impoverished. The Eisenhowers then lived in Texas from 1889 until 1892, and later returned to Kansas, with $24 to their name at the time. David worked as a railroad mechanic and then at a creamery. By 1898, the parents made a decent living and provided a suitable home for their large family.

The future president was born on October 14, 1890, in Denison, Texas, the third of seven boys. His mother originally named him David Dwight but reversed the two names after his birth to avoid the confusion of having two Davids in the family. All of the boys were called "Ike", such as "Big Ike"

(Edgar) and "Little Ike" (Dwight); the nickname was intended as an abbreviation of their last name. By World War II, only Dwight was still called "Ike".

In 1892, the family moved to Abilene, Kansas, which Eisenhower considered his hometown. As a child, he was involved in an accident that cost his younger brother an eye; he later referred to this as an experience that taught him the need to be protective of those under him.Wikipedia:Citation needed Dwight developed a keen and enduring interest in exploring outdoors, hunting/fishing, cooking and card playing from an illiterate named Bob Davis who camped on the Smoky Hill River.[3]

While Eisenhower's mother was against war, it was her collection of history books that first sparked Eisenhower's early and lasting interest in military history. He persisted in reading the books in her collection and became a voracious reader on the subject. Other favorite subjects early in his education were arithmetic and spelling.

His parents set aside specific times at breakfast and at dinner for daily family Bible reading. Chores were regularly assigned and rotated among all the children, and misbehavior was met with unequivocal discipline, usually from David. His mother, previously a member (with David) of the River Brethren sect of the Mennonites, joined the International Bible Students Association, later known as Jehovah's Witnesses. The Eisenhower home served as the local meeting hall from 1896 to 1915, though Eisenhower never joined the International Bible Students.[4] His later decision to attend West Point saddened his mother, who felt that warfare was "rather wicked", but she did not overrule him.[5] While speaking of himself in 1948, Eisenhower said he was "one of the most deeply religious men I know" though unattached to any "sect or organization". He was baptized in the Presbyterian Church in 1953.[6]

Eisenhower attended Abilene High School and graduated with the class of 1909. As a freshman, he injured his knee and developed a leg infection that extended into his groin, and which his doctor diagnosed as life-threatening. The doctor insisted that the leg be amputated but Dwight refused to allow it, and surprisingly recovered, though he had to repeat his freshman year. He and brother Edgar both wanted to attend college, though they lacked the funds. They made a pact to take alternate years at college while the other worked to earn the tuitions.

Edgar took the first turn at school, and Dwight was employed as a night supervisor at the Belle Springs Creamery. When Edgar asked for a second year, Dwight consented and worked for a second year. At that time, a friend "Swede" Hazlett was applying to the Naval Academy and urged Dwight to apply to the school, since no tuition was required. Eisenhower requested consideration for either Annapolis or West Point with his U.S. Senator, Joseph L.

Figure 2: *Eisenhower (second from left) and Omar Bradley (second from right) were members of the 1912 West Point football team.*

Bristow. Though Eisenhower was among the winners of the entrance-exam competition, he was beyond the age limit for the Naval Academy. He then accepted an appointment to West Point in 1911.

At West Point, Eisenhower relished the emphasis on traditions and on sports, but was less enthusiastic about the hazing, though he willingly accepted it as a plebe. He was also a regular violator of the more detailed regulations, and finished school with a less than stellar discipline rating. Academically, Eisenhower's best subject by far was English. Otherwise, his performance was average, though he thoroughly enjoyed the typical emphasis of engineering on science and mathematics.

In athletics, Eisenhower later said that "not making the baseball team at West Point was one of the greatest disappointments of my life, maybe my greatest". He made the varsity football team and was a starter as running back and linebacker in 1912, when he tackled the legendary Jim Thorpe of the Carlisle Indians. Eisenhower suffered a torn knee while being tackled in the next game, which was the last he played; he re-injured his knee on horseback and in the boxing ring,[7] so he turned to fencing and gymnastics.

Eisenhower later served as junior varsity football coach and cheerleader. He graduated in the middle of the class of 1915, which became known as "the class the stars fell on", because 59 members eventually became general officers.

Figure 3: *Mamie Eisenhower, painted in 1953 by Thomas Stevens*

Personal life

While Eisenhower was stationed in Texas, he met Mamie Doud of Boone, Iowa. They were immediately taken with each other. He proposed to her on Valentine's Day in 1916. A November wedding date in Denver was moved up to July 1 due to the pending U.S. entry into World War I. They moved many times during their first 35 years of marriage.

The Eisenhowers had two sons. Doud Dwight "Icky" Eisenhower (1917–1921) died of scarlet fever at the age of three. Eisenhower was mostly reticent to discuss his death. Their second son, John Eisenhower (1922–2013), was born in Denver, Colorado. John served in the United States Army, retired as a brigadier general, became an author and served as U.S. Ambassador to Belgium from 1969 to 1971. Coincidentally, John graduated from West Point on D-Day, June 6, 1944. He married Barbara Jean Thompson on June 10, 1947. John and Barbara had four children: David, Barbara Ann, Susan Elaine and Mary Jean. David, after whom Camp David is named, married Richard Nixon's daughter Julie in 1968.

Eisenhower was a golf enthusiast later in life, and he joined the Augusta National Golf Club in 1948.[8] He played golf frequently during and after his presidency and was unreserved in expressing his passion for the game, to the point of golfing during winter; he ordered his golf balls painted black so he could see them better against snow on the ground. He had a small, basic golf facility installed at Camp David, and became close friends with the Augusta National Chairman Clifford Roberts, inviting Roberts to stay at the White House on several occasions. Roberts, an investment broker, also handled the Eisenhower family's investments. Roberts also advised Eisenhower on tax aspects of publishing his memoirs, which proved financially lucrative.

Oil painting was one of Eisenhower's hobbies. He began painting while at Columbia University, after watching Thomas E. Stephens paint Mamie's portrait. In order to relax, Eisenhower painted about 260 oils during the last 20 years of his life. The images were mostly landscapes, but also portraits of subjects such as Mamie, their grandchildren, General Montgomery, George Washington, and Abraham Lincoln. Wendy Beckett stated that Eisenhower's work, "simple and earnest, rather cause us to wonder at the hidden depths of this reticent president". A conservative in both art and politics, he in a 1962 speech denounced modern art as "a piece of canvas that looks like a broken-down Tin Lizzie, loaded with paint, has been driven over it".

Angels in the Outfield was Eisenhower's favorite movie. His favorite reading material for relaxation were the Western novels of Zane Grey. With his excellent memory and ability to focus, Eisenhower was skilled at card games. He learned poker, which he called his "favorite indoor sport", in Abilene. Eisenhower recorded West Point classmates' poker losses for payment after graduation, and later stopped playing because his opponents resented having to pay him. A friend reported that after learning to play contract bridge at West Point, Eisenhower played the game six nights a week for five months. Eisenhower continued to play bridge throughout his military career. While stationed in the Philippines, he played regularly with President Manuel Quezon, and was dubbed "The bridge wizard of Manila". During WWII, an unwritten qualification for an officer's appointment to Eisenhower's staff was the ability to play a sound game of bridge. He played even during the stressful weeks leading up to the D-Day landings. His favorite partner was General Alfred Gruenther, considered the best player in the U.S. Army; he appointed Gruenther his second-in-command at NATO partly because of his skill at bridge. Saturday night bridge games at the White House were a feature of his presidency. He was a strong player, though not an expert by modern standards. The great bridge player and popularizer Ely Culbertson described his game as classic and sound with "flashes of brilliance", and said that "You can always judge a man's character by the way he plays cards. Eisenhower is a calm and collected player and never whines at his losses. He is brilliant in victory but never commits the bridge player's worst crime of gloating when he wins." Bridge expert Oswald Jacoby frequently participated in the White House games, and said, "The President plays better bridge than golf. He tries to break 90 at golf. At bridge, you would say he plays in the 70s."

World War I

After graduation in 1915, Second Lieutenant Eisenhower requested an assignment in the Philippines, which was denied. He served initially in logistics and then the infantry at various camps in Texas and Georgia until 1918. In 1916, while stationed at Fort Sam Houston, Eisenhower was football coach for St. Louis College, now St. Mary's University.[9] Eisenhower was an honorary member of the Sigma Beta Chi fraternity at St. Mary's University. In late 1917, while in charge of training at Ft. Oglethorpe in Georgia, his wife Mamie had their first son.

When the U.S. entered World War I, he immediately requested an overseas assignment but was again denied and then assigned to Ft. Leavenworth, Kansas. In February 1918, he was transferred to Camp Meade in Maryland with the 65th Engineers. His unit was later ordered to France, but to his chagrin he received orders for the new tank corps, where he was promoted to brevet lieutenant colonel in the National Army.[10] He commanded a unit that trained tank crews at Camp Colt – his first command – at the site of "Pickett's Charge" on the Gettysburg, Pennsylvania Civil War battleground. Though Eisenhower and his tank crews never saw combat, he displayed excellent organizational skills, as well as an ability to accurately assess junior officers' strengths and make optimal placements of personnel.

Once again his spirits were raised when the unit under his command received orders overseas to France. This time his wishes were thwarted when the armistice was signed a week before his departure date. Completely missing out on the warfront left him depressed and bitter for a time, despite receiving the Distinguished Service Medal for his work at home.Wikipedia:Citation needed In World War II, rivals who had combat service in the first great war (led by Gen. Bernard Montgomery) sought to denigrate Eisenhower for his previous lack of combat duty, despite his stateside experience establishing a camp, completely equipped, for thousands of troops, and developing a full combat training schedule.

In service of generals

After the war, Eisenhower reverted to his regular rank of captain and a few days later was promoted to major, a rank he held for 16 years. The major was assigned in 1919 to a transcontinental Army convoy to test vehicles and dramatize the need for improved roads in the nation. Indeed, the convoy averaged only 5 mph from Washington, D.C., to San Francisco; later the improvement of highways became a signature issue for Eisenhower as President.

He assumed duties again at Camp Meade, Maryland, commanding a battalion of tanks, where he remained until 1922. His schooling continued, focused on

Figure 4: *Eisenhower (far right) with three unidentified men in 1919, four years after graduating from West Point*

the nature of the next war and the role of the tank in it. His new expertise in tank warfare was strengthened by a close collaboration with George S. Patton, Sereno E. Brett, and other senior tank leaders. Their leading-edge ideas of speed-oriented offensive tank warfare were strongly discouraged by superiors, who considered the new approach too radical and preferred to continue using tanks in a strictly supportive role for the infantry. Eisenhower was even threatened with court-martial for continued publication of these proposed methods of tank deployment, and he relented.

From 1920, Eisenhower served under a succession of talented generals – Fox Conner, John J. Pershing, Douglas MacArthur and George Marshall. He first became executive officer to General Conner in the Panama Canal Zone, where, joined by Mamie, he served until 1924. Under Conner's tutelage, he studied military history and theory (including Carl von Clausewitz's *On War*), and later cited Conner's enormous influence on his military thinking, saying in 1962 that "Fox Conner was the ablest man I ever knew." Conner's comment on Eisenhower was, "[He] is one of the most capable, efficient and loyal officers I have ever met." On Conner's recommendation, in 1925–26 he attended the Command and General Staff College at Fort Leavenworth, Kansas, where he graduated first in a class of 245 officers.[11] He then served as a battalion commander at Fort Benning, Georgia, until 1927.

During the late 1920s and early 1930s, Eisenhower's career in the post-war army stalled somewhat, as military priorities diminished; many of his friends resigned for high-paying business jobs. He was assigned to the American Battle Monuments Commission directed by General Pershing, and with the help of his brother Milton Eisenhower, then a journalist at the Agriculture Department, he produced a guide to American battlefields in Europe. He then was assigned to the Army War College and graduated in 1928. After a one-year assignment in France, Eisenhower served as executive officer to General George V. Mosely, Assistant Secretary of War, from 1929 to February 1933. Major Dwight D. Eisenhower graduated from the Army Industrial College (Washington, DC) in 1933 and later served on the faculty (it was later expanded to become the Industrial College of the Armed Services and is now known as the Dwight D. Eisenhower School for National Security and Resource Strategy).

His primary duty was planning for the next war, which proved most difficult in the midst of the Great Depression. He then was posted as chief military aide to General Douglas MacArthur, Army Chief of Staff. In 1932, he participated in the clearing of the Bonus March encampment in Washington, D.C. Although he was against the actions taken against the veterans and strongly advised MacArthur against taking a public role in it, he later wrote the Army's official incident report, endorsing MacArthur's conduct.

In 1935, he accompanied MacArthur to the Philippines, where he served as assistant military adviser to the Philippine government in developing their army. Eisenhower had strong philosophical disagreements with MacArthur regarding the role of the Philippine Army and the leadership qualities that an American army officer should exhibit and develop in his subordinates. The resulting antipathy between Eisenhower and MacArthur lasted the rest of their lives.[12]

Historians have concluded that this assignment provided valuable preparation for handling the challenging personalities of Winston Churchill, George S. Patton, George Marshall, and General Montgomery during World War II. Eisenhower later emphasized that too much had been made of the disagreements with MacArthur, and that a positive relationship endured. While in Manila, Mamie suffered a life-threatening stomach ailment but recovered fully. Eisenhower was promoted to the rank of permanent lieutenant colonel in 1936. He also learned to fly, making a solo flight over the Philippines in 1937, and obtained his private pilot's license in 1939 at Fort Lewis. Also around this time, he was offered a post by the Philippine Commonwealth Government, namely by then Philippine President Manuel L. Quezon on recommendations by MacArthur, to become the chief of police of a new capital being planned, now named Quezon City, but he declined the offer.

Eisenhower returned to the United States in December 1939 and was assigned as commanding officer (CO) of the 1st Battalion, 15th Infantry Regiment at

Fort Lewis, Washington, later becoming the regimental executive officer. In March 1941 he was promoted to colonel and assigned as chief of staff of the newly activated IX Corps under Major General Kenyon Joyce. In June 1941, he was appointed chief of staff to General Walter Krueger, Commander of the Third Army, at Fort Sam Houston in San Antonio, Texas. After successfully participating in the Louisiana Maneuvers, he was promoted to brigadier general on October 3, 1941.[13] Although his administrative abilities had been noticed, on the eve of the American entry into World War II he had never held an active command above a battalion and was far from being considered by many as a potential commander of major operations.

World War II

After the Japanese attack on Pearl Harbor, Eisenhower was assigned to the General Staff in Washington, where he served until June 1942 with responsibility for creating the major war plans to defeat Japan and Germany. He was appointed Deputy Chief in charge of Pacific Defenses under the Chief of War Plans Division (WPD), General Leonard T. Gerow, and then succeeded Gerow as Chief of the War Plans Division. Next, he was appointed Assistant Chief of Staff in charge of the new Operations Division (which replaced WPD) under Chief of Staff General George C. Marshall, who spotted talent and promoted accordingly.

At the end of May 1942, Eisenhower accompanied Lt. Gen. Henry H. Arnold, commanding general of the Army Air Forces, to London to assess the effectiveness of the theater commander in England, Maj. Gen. James E. Chaney. He returned to Washington on June 3 with a pessimistic assessment, stating he had an "uneasy feeling" about Chaney and his staff. On June 23, 1942, he returned to London as Commanding General, European Theater of Operations (ETOUSA), based in London and with a house on Coombe, Kingston upon Thames,[14] and took over command of ETOUSA from Chaney. He was promoted to lieutenant general on July 7.

Operations Torch and Avalanche

In November 1942, he was also appointed Supreme Commander Allied Expeditionary Force of the North African Theater of Operations (NATOUSA) through the new operational Headquarters Allied (Expeditionary) Force Headquarters (A(E)FHQ). The word "expeditionary" was dropped soon after his appointment for security reasons.Wikipedia:Verifiability The campaign in North Africa was designated Operation Torch and was planned underground within the Rock of Gibraltar. Eisenhower was the first non-British person to command Gibraltar in 200 years.

Figure 5: *Eisenhower as a major general, 1942*

Figure 6: *Eisenhower as General of the Army, 1945*

French cooperation was deemed necessary to the campaign, and Eisenhower encountered a "preposterous situation" with the multiple rival factions in France. His primary objective was to move forces successfully into Tunisia, and intending to facilitate that objective, he gave his support to François Darlan as High Commissioner in North Africa, despite Darlan's previous high offices of state in Vichy France and his continued role as commander-in-chief of the French armed forces. The Allied leaders were "thunderstruck" by this from a political standpoint, though none of them had offered Eisenhower guidance with the problem in the course of planning the operation. Eisenhower was severely criticized for the move. Darlan was assassinated on December 24 by Fernand Bonnier de La Chapelle. Eisenhower did not take action to prevent the arrest and extrajudicial execution of Bonnier de La Chapelle by associates of Darlan acting without authority from either Vichy or the Allies, considering it a criminal rather than a military matter.[15] Eisenhower later appointed, as High Commissioner, General Henri Giraud, who had been installed by the Allies as Darlan's commander-in-chief, and who had refused to postpone the execution.

Operation Torch also served as a valuable training ground for Eisenhower's combat command skills; during the initial phase of *Generalfeldmarschall* Erwin Rommel's move into the Kasserine Pass, Eisenhower created some confusion in the ranks by some interference with the execution of battle plans by his subordinates. He also was initially indecisive in his removal of Lloyd Fredendall, commanding U.S. II Corps. He became more adroit in such matters in later campaigns.[16] In February 1943, his authority was extended as commander of AFHQ across the Mediterranean basin to include the British Eighth Army, commanded by General Sir Bernard Montgomery. The Eighth Army had advanced across the Western Desert from the east and was ready for the start of the Tunisia Campaign. Eisenhower gained his fourth star and gave up command of ETOUSA to become commander of NATOUSA.

After the capitulation of Axis forces in North Africa, Eisenhower oversaw the invasion of Sicily. Once Mussolini, the Italian leader, had fallen in Italy, the Allies switched their attention to the mainland with Operation Avalanche. But while Eisenhower argued with President Roosevelt and British Prime Minister Churchill, who both insisted on unconditional terms of surrender in exchange for helping the Italians, the Germans pursued an aggressive buildup of forces in the country. The Germans made the already tough battle more difficult by adding 19 divisions and initially outnumbering the Allied forces 2 to 1.

Figure 7: *General Eisenhower, General Patton and President Roosevelt in Sicily, 1943*

Supreme Allied commander and Operation Overlord

In December 1943, President Roosevelt decided that Eisenhower – not Marshall – would be Supreme Allied Commander in Europe. The following month, he resumed command of ETOUSA and the following month was officially designated as the Supreme Allied Commander of the Allied Expeditionary Force (SHAEF), serving in a dual role until the end of hostilities in Europe in May 1945. He was charged in these positions with planning and carrying out the Allied assault on the coast of Normandy in June 1944 under the code name Operation Overlord, the liberation of Western Europe and the invasion of Germany.

Eisenhower, as well as the officers and troops under him, had learned valuable lessons in their previous operations, and their skills had all strengthened in preparation for the next most difficult campaign against the Germans—a beach landing assault. His first struggles, however, were with Allied leaders and officers on matters vital to the success of the Normandy invasion; he argued with Roosevelt over an essential agreement with De Gaulle to use French resistance forces in covert and sabotage operations against the Germans in advance of Overlord. Admiral Ernest J. King fought with Eisenhower over King's refusal to provide additional landing craft from the Pacific. He also insisted that the

Figure 8: *Eisenhower speaks with men of the 502nd Parachute Infantry Regiment, part of the 101st Airborne Division, on June 5, 1944, the day before the D-Day invasion.*

British give him exclusive command over all strategic air forces to facilitate Overlord, to the point of threatening to resign unless Churchill relented, as he did. Eisenhower then designed a bombing plan in France in advance of Overlord and argued with Churchill over the latter's concern with civilian casualties; de Gaulle interjected that the casualties were justified in shedding the yoke of the Germans, and Eisenhower prevailed. He also had to skillfully manage to retain the services of the often unruly George S. Patton, by severely reprimanding him when Patton earlier had slapped a subordinate, and then when Patton gave a speech in which he made improper comments about postwar policy.

The D-Day Normandy landings on June 6, 1944, were costly but successful. Two months later (August 15), the invasion of Southern France took place, and control of forces in the southern invasion passed from the AFHQ to the SHAEF. Many thought that victory in Europe would come by summer's end, but the Germans did not capitulate for almost a year. From then until the end of the war in Europe on May 8, 1945, Eisenhower, through SHAEF, commanded all Allied forces, and through his command of ETOUSA had administrative command of all U.S. forces on the Western Front north of the Alps. He was ever mindful of the inevitable loss of life and suffering that would be experienced on an individual level by the troops under his command and their

Figure 9: *From left, front row includes army officers Simpson, Patton, Spaatz, Eisenhower, Bradley, Hodges and Gerow in 1945*

families. This prompted him to make a point of visiting every division involved in the invasion. Eisenhower's sense of responsibility was underscored by his draft of a statement to be issued if the invasion failed. It has been called one of the great speeches of history:

> *Our landings in the Cherbourg-Havre area have failed to gain a satisfactory foothold and I have withdrawn the troops. My decision to attack at this time and place was based on the best information available. The troops, the air and the Navy did all that bravery and devotion to duty could do. If any blame or fault attaches to the attempt, it is mine alone.*[17]

Liberation of France and victory in Europe

Once the coastal assault had succeeded, Eisenhower insisted on retaining personal control over the land battle strategy, and was immersed in the command and supply of multiple assaults through France on Germany. Field Marshal Montgomery insisted priority be given to his 21st Army Group's attack being made in the north, while Generals Bradley (12th U.S. Army Group) and Devers (Sixth U.S. Army Group) insisted they be given priority in the center and south of the front (respectively). Eisenhower worked tirelessly to address the demands of the rival commanders to optimize Allied forces, often by giving

Figure 10: *Eisenhower with Allied commanders following the signing of the German Instrument of Surrender at Reims*

them tactical latitude; many historians conclude this delayed the Allied victory in Europe. However, due to Eisenhower's persistence, the pivotal supply port at Antwerp was successfully, albeit belatedly, opened in late 1944, and victory became a more distinct probability.

In recognition of his senior position in the Allied command, on December 20, 1944, he was promoted to General of the Army, equivalent to the rank of Field Marshal in most European armies. In this and the previous high commands he held, Eisenhower showed his great talents for leadership and diplomacy. Although he had never seen action himself, he won the respect of front-line commanders. He interacted adeptly with allies such as Winston Churchill, Field Marshal Bernard Montgomery and General Charles de Gaulle. He had serious disagreements with Churchill and Montgomery over questions of strategy, but these rarely upset his relationships with them. He dealt with Soviet Marshal Zhukov, his Russian counterpart, and they became good friends.[18]

In December 1944, The Germans launched a surprise counter offensive, the Battle of the Bulge, which the Allies turned back in early 1945 after Eisenhower repositioned his armies and improved weather allowed the Air Force to engage. German defenses continued to deteriorate on both the eastern front with the Soviets and the western front with the Allies. The British wanted to capture Berlin, but Eisenhower decided it would be a military mistake for him to attack Berlin, and said orders to that effect would have to be explicit. The

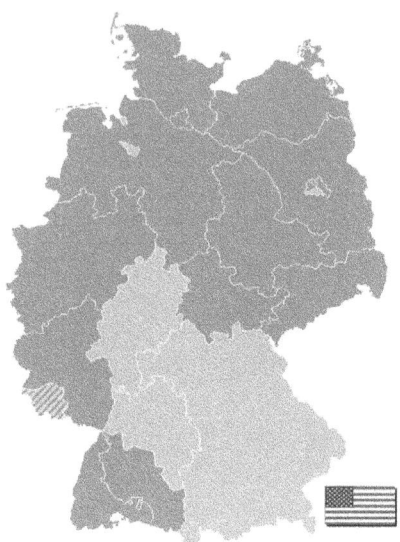

Figure 11: *General Eisenhower served as military governor of the American zone (highlighted) in Allied-occupied Germany from May through November 1945*

British backed down, but then wanted Eisenhower to move into Czechoslovakia for political reasons. Washington refused to support Churchill's plan to use Eisenhower's army for political maneuvers against Moscow. The actual division of Germany followed the lines that Roosevelt, Churchill and Stalin had previously agreed upon. The Soviet Red Army captured Berlin in a very large-scale bloody battle, and the Germans finally surrendered on May 7, 1945.

In 1945, Eisenhower anticipated that someday an attempt would be made to recharacterize Nazi crimes as propaganda (Holocaust denial) and took steps against it by demanding extensive still and movie photographic documentation of Nazi death camps.

After World War II

Military Governor in Germany and Army Chief of Staff

Following the German unconditional surrender, Eisenhower was appointed military governor of the American occupation zone, located primarily in Southern Germany, and headquartered at the IG Farben Building in Frankfurt am Main. Upon discovery of the Nazi concentration camps, he ordered camera crews to document evidence of the atrocities in them for use in the

Figure 12: *General Eisenhower (left) in Warsaw, Poland, 1945*

Nuremberg Trials. He reclassified German prisoners of war (POWs) in U.S. custody as Disarmed Enemy Forces (DEFs), who were no longer subject to the Geneva Convention. Eisenhower followed the orders laid down by the Joint Chiefs of Staff (JCS) in directive JCS 1067, but softened them by bringing in 400,000 tons of food for civilians and allowing more fraternization.[19,20,21] In response to the devastation in Germany, including food shortages and an influx of refugees, he arranged distribution of American food and medical equipment.[22] His actions reflected the new American attitudes of the German people as Nazi victims not villains, while aggressively purging the ex-Nazis.[23,24]

In November 1945, Eisenhower returned to Washington to replace Marshall as Chief of Staff of the Army. His main role was rapid demobilization of millions of soldiers, a slow job that was delayed by lack of shipping. Eisenhower was convinced in 1946 that the Soviet Union did not want war and that friendly relations could be maintained; he strongly supported the new United Nations and favored its involvement in the control of atomic bombs. However, in formulating policies regarding the atomic bomb and relations with the Soviets, Truman was guided by the U.S. State Department and ignored Eisenhower and the Pentagon. Indeed, Eisenhower had opposed the use of the atomic bomb against the Japanese, writing, "First, the Japanese were ready to surrender and it wasn't necessary to hit them with that awful thing. Second, I hated to see our country be the first to use such a weapon."[25] Initially, Eisenhower hoped for cooperation with the Soviets. He even visited Warsaw in 1945. Invited by Bolesław Bierut and decorated with the highest military decoration, he was shocked by the scale of destruction in the city. However, by mid-1947, as East–West tensions over economic recovery in Germany and the Greek Civil War escalated, Eisenhower agreed with a containment policy to stop Soviet expansion.

1948 presidential election

In June 1943, a visiting politician had suggested to Eisenhower that he might become President of the United States after the war. Believing that a general should not participate in politics, one author later wrote that "figuratively speaking, [Eisenhower] kicked his political-minded visitor out of his office". As others asked him about his political future, Eisenhower told one that he could not imagine wanting to be considered for any political job "from dog-catcher to Grand High Supreme King of the Universe", and another that he could not serve as Army Chief of Staff if others believed he had political ambitions. In 1945 Truman told Eisenhower during the Potsdam Conference that if desired, the president would help the general win the 1948 election, and in 1947 he offered to run as Eisenhower's running mate on the Democratic ticket if MacArthur won the Republican nomination.[26]

As the election approached, other prominent citizens and politicians from both parties urged Eisenhower to run for president. In January 1948, after learning of plans in New Hampshire to elect delegates supporting him for the forthcoming Republican National Convention, Eisenhower stated through the Army that he was "not available for and could not accept nomination to high political office"; "life-long professional soldiers", he wrote, "in the absence of some obvious and overriding reason, [should] abstain from seeking high political office". Eisenhower maintained no political party affiliation during this time. Many believed he was forgoing his only opportunity to be president: Republican Thomas E. Dewey was considered the probable winner and would presumably serve two terms, meaning that Eisenhower, at age 66 in 1956, would be too old to have another chance to run.

President at Columbia University and NATO Supreme Commander

In 1948, Eisenhower became President of Columbia University, an Ivy League university in New York City, where he was inducted into Phi Beta Kappa. The assignment was described as not being a good fit in either direction.[27] During that year Eisenhower's memoir, *Crusade in Europe*, was published.[28] Critics regarded it as one of the finest U.S. military memoirs, and it was a major

Figure 13: *The Supreme Commanders of the Four Powers on June 5, 1945, in Berlin: Bernard Montgomery, Dwight D. Eisenhower, Georgy Zhukov and Jean de Lattre de Tassigny*

financial success as well. Eisenhower's profit on the book was substantially aided by an unprecedented ruling by the U.S. Department of the Treasury that Eisenhower was not a professional writer, but rather, marketing the lifetime asset of his experiences, and thus he had to pay only capital gains tax on his $635,000 advance instead of the much higher personal tax rate. This ruling saved Eisenhower about $400,000.[29]

Eisenhower's stint as the president of Columbia University was punctuated by his activity within the Council on Foreign Relations, a study group he led as president concerning the political and military implications of the Marshall Plan, and The American Assembly, Eisenhower's "vision of a great cultural center where business, professional and governmental leaders could meet from time to time to discuss and reach conclusions concerning problems of a social and political nature". His biographer Blanche Wiesen Cook suggested that this period served as "the political education of General Eisenhower", since he had to prioritize wide-ranging educational, administrative, and financial demands for the university. Through his involvement in the Council on Foreign Relations, he also gained exposure to economic analysis, which would become the bedrock of his understanding in economic policy. "Whatever General Eisenhower knows about economics, he has learned at the study group meetings," one Aid to Europe member claimed.

Eisenhower accepted the presidency of the university to expand his ability to promote "the American form of democracy" through education. He was clear on this point to the trustees involved in the search committee. He informed them that his main purpose was "to promote the basic concepts of education in a democracy". As a result, he was "almost incessantly" devoted to the idea of the American Assembly, a concept he developed into an institution by the end of 1950.

Within months of beginning his tenure as the president of the university, Eisenhower was requested to advise U.S. Secretary of Defense James Forrestal on the unification of the armed services. About six months after his appointment, he became the informal Chairman of the Joint Chiefs of Staff in Washington. Two months later he fell ill, and he spent over a month in recovery at the Augusta National Golf Club. He returned to his post in New York in mid-May, and in July 1949 took a two-month vacation out-of-state. Because the American Assembly had begun to take shape, he traveled around the country during mid-to-late 1950, building financial support from Columbia Associates, an alumni association.

Eisenhower was unknowingly building resentment and a reputation among the Columbia University faculty and staff as an absentee president who was using the university for his own interests. As a career military man, he naturally had little in common with the academics.

The contacts gained through university and American Assembly fund-raising activities would later become important supporters in Eisenhower's bid for the Republican party nomination and the presidency. Meanwhile, Columbia University's liberal faculty members became disenchanted with the university president's ties to oilmen and businessmen, including Leonard McCollum, the president of Continental Oil; Frank Abrams, the chairman of Standard Oil of New Jersey; Bob Kleberg, the president of the King Ranch; H. J. Porter, a Texas oil executive; Bob Woodruff, the president of the Coca-Cola Corporation; and Clarence Francis, the chairman of General Foods.

As the president of Columbia, Eisenhower gave voice and form to his opinions about the supremacy and difficulties of American democracy. His tenure marked his transformation from military to civilian leadership. His biographer Travis Beal Jacobs also suggested that the alienation of the Columbia faculty contributed to sharp intellectual criticism of him for many years.[30]

The trustees of Columbia University refused to accept Eisenhower's resignation in December 1950, when he took an extended leave from the university to become the Supreme Commander of the North Atlantic Treaty Organization (NATO), and he was given operational command of NATO forces in Europe.

Figure 14: *Button from the 1952 campaign*

Eisenhower retired from active service as an army general on May 31, 1952, and he resumed his presidency of Columbia. He held this position until January 20, 1953, when he became the President of the United States.

NATO did not have strong bipartisan support in Congress at the time that Eisenhower assumed its military command. Eisenhower advised the participating European nations that it would be incumbent upon them to demonstrate their own commitment of troops and equipment to the NATO force before such would come from the war-weary United States.

At home, Eisenhower was more effective in making the case for NATO in Congress than the Truman administration had been. By the middle of 1951, with American and European support, NATO was a genuine military power. Nevertheless, Eisenhower thought that NATO would become a truly European alliance, with the American and Canadian commitments ending after about ten years.

Presidential campaign of 1952

President Truman, symbolizing a broad-based desire for an Eisenhower candidacy for president, again in 1951 pressed him to run for the office as a Democrat. It was at this time that Eisenhower voiced his disagreements with the Democratic Party and declared himself and his family to be Republicans. A

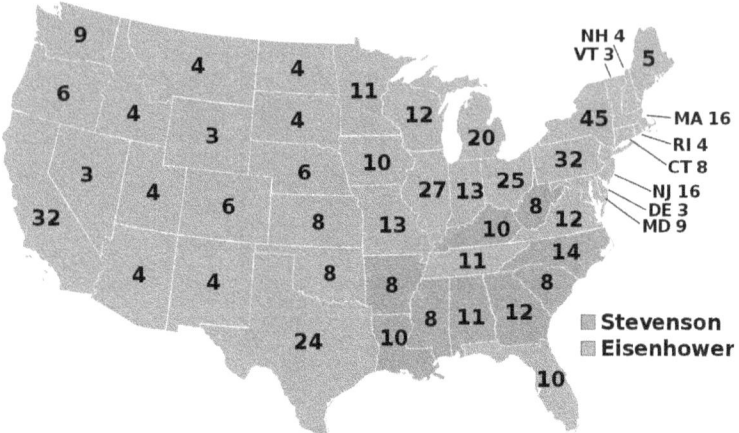

Figure 15: *1952 electoral vote results*

"Draft Eisenhower" movement in the Republican Party persuaded him to declare his candidacy in the 1952 presidential election to counter the candidacy of non-interventionist Senator Robert A. Taft. The effort was a long struggle; Eisenhower had to be convinced that political circumstances had created a genuine duty for him to offer himself as a candidate, and that there was a mandate from the populace for him to be their President. Henry Cabot Lodge, who served as his campaign manager, and others succeeded in convincing him, and in June 1952 he resigned his command at NATO to campaign full-time. Eisenhower defeated Taft for the nomination, having won critical delegate votes from Texas. Eisenhower's campaign was noted for the simple but effective slogan, "I Like Ike". It was essential to his success that Eisenhower express opposition to Roosevelt's policy at Yalta and against Truman's policies in Korea and China—matters in which he had once participated. In defeating Taft for the nomination, it became necessary for Eisenhower to appease the right wing Old Guard of the Republican Party; his selection of Richard M. Nixon as the Vice-President on the ticket was designed in part for that purpose. Nixon also provided a strong anti-communist presence as well as some youth to counter Ike's more advanced age.

In the general election, against the advice of his advisers, Eisenhower insisted on campaigning in the South, refusing to surrender the region to the Democratic Party. The campaign strategy, dubbed "K_1C_2", was to focus on attacking the Truman and Roosevelt administrations on three issues: Korea, Communism and corruption. In an effort to accommodate the right, he stressed that the liberation of Eastern Europe should be by peaceful means only; he also distanced himself from his former boss President Truman.

Figure 16: *Presidential candidate Eisenhower in the Hobo Day parade at South Dakota State University in 1952*

Two controversies during the campaign tested him and his staff, but did not affect the campaign. One involved a report that Nixon had improperly received funds from a secret trust. Nixon spoke out adroitly to avoid potential damage, but the matter permanently alienated the two candidates. The second issue centered on Eisenhower's relented decision to confront the controversial methods of Joseph McCarthy on his home turf in a Wisconsin appearance.[31] Just two weeks prior to the election, Eisenhower vowed to go to Korea and end the war there. He promised to maintain a strong commitment against Communism while avoiding the topic of NATO; finally, he stressed a corruption-free, frugal administration at home.

He defeated Democratic candidate Adlai Stevenson II in a landslide, with an electoral margin of 442 to 89, marking the first Republican return to the White House in 20 years. In the election he also brought with him a Republican majority in the House (by eight votes) and in the Senate (actually a tie, with Nixon providing the majority vote).

Eisenhower was the last president born in the 19th century, and at age 62, was the oldest man elected President since James Buchanan in 1856 (President Truman stood at 64 in 1948 as the incumbent president, having succeeded to the Presidency in 1945 upon the death of Franklin Roosevelt). Eisenhower was the only general to serve as President in the 20th century and was the most recent President to have never held elected office prior to the Presidency until Donald Trump, who never held public office nor served in the military;

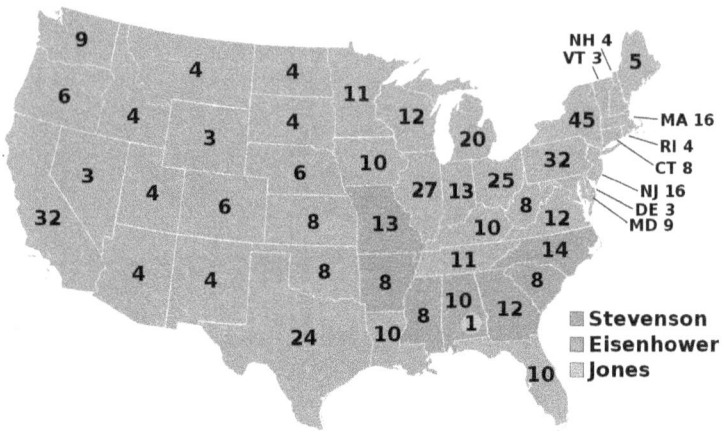

Figure 17: *1956 electoral vote results*

the other Presidents who did not have prior elected office were Zachary Taylor, Ulysses S. Grant, William Howard Taft, and Herbert Hoover.

Election of 1956

The United States presidential election of 1956 was held on November 6, 1956. Eisenhower, the popular incumbent, successfully ran for re-election. The election was a re-match of 1952, as his opponent in 1956 was Stevenson, a former Illinois governor, whom Eisenhower had defeated four years earlier. Compared to the 1952 election, Eisenhower gained Kentucky, Louisiana, and West Virginia from Stevenson, while losing Missouri. His voters were less likely to bring up his leadership record. Instead what stood out this time, "was the response to personal qualities— to his sincerity, his integrity and sense of duty, his virtue as a family man, his religious devotion, and his sheer likeableness."

Presidency (1953–1961)

Due to a complete estrangement between the two as a result of campaigning, Truman and Eisenhower had minimal discussions about the transition of administrations. After selecting his budget director, Joseph M. Dodge, Eisenhower asked Herbert Brownell Jr. and Lucius D. Clay to make recommendations for his cabinet appointments. He accepted their recommendations without exception; they included John Foster Dulles and George M. Humphrey with whom he developed his closest relationships, and one woman, Oveta Culp Hobby. Eisenhower's cabinet, consisting of several corporate executives

Figure 18: *February 1959 White House Portrait*

and one labor leader, was dubbed by one journalist, "Eight millionaires and a plumber." The cabinet was known for its lack of personal friends, office seekers, or experienced government administrators. He also upgraded the role of the National Security Council in planning all phases of the Cold War.

Prior to his inauguration, Eisenhower led a meeting of advisors at Pearl Harbor addressing foremost issues; agreed objectives were to balance the budget during his term, to bring the Korean War to an end, to defend vital interests at lower cost through nuclear deterrent, and to end price and wage controls. Eisenhower also conducted the first pre-inaugural cabinet meeting in history in late 1952; he used this meeting to articulate his anti-communist Russia policy. His inaugural address was also exclusively devoted to foreign policy and included this same philosophy as well as a commitment to foreign trade and the United Nations.

Eisenhower made greater use of press conferences than any previous president, holding almost 200 over his two terms. While he saw the benefit of maintaining a good relationship with the press, he saw more value in them as a means of direct communication with the American people.

Throughout his presidency, Eisenhower adhered to a political philosophy of dynamic conservatism. A self-described "progressive conservative" who used terms like "progressive moderate" and "dynamic conservatism" to describe his approach, he continued all the major New Deal programs still in operation, especially Social Security. He expanded its programs and rolled them into a new cabinet-level agency, the Department of Health, Education and Welfare, while extending benefits to an additional ten million workers. He implemented integration in the Armed Services in two years, which had not been completed under Truman.

When the 1954 Congressional elections approached, it became evident that the Republicans were in danger of losing their thin majority in both houses. Eisenhower was among those who blamed the Old Guard for the losses, and he took up the charge to stop suspected efforts by the right wing to take control of the GOP. Eisenhower then articulated his position as a moderate, progressive Republican: "I have just one purpose ... and that is to build up a strong progressive Republican Party in this country. If the right wing wants a fight, they are going to get it ... before I end up, either this Republican Party will reflect progressivism or I won't be with them anymore."

Eisenhower initially planned on serving only one term, but as with other decisions, he maintained a position of maximum flexibility in case leading Republicans wanted him to run again. During his recovery from a heart attack late in 1955, he huddled with his closest advisors to evaluate the GOP's potential candidates; the group, in addition to his doctor, concluded a second term was well advised, and he announced in February 1956 he would run again. Eisenhower was publicly noncommittal about Nixon's repeating as the Vice President on his ticket; the question was an especially important one in light of his heart condition. He personally favored Robert B. Anderson, a Democrat, who rejected his offer; Eisenhower then resolved to leave the matter in the hands of the party. In 1956, Eisenhower faced Adlai Stevenson again and won by an even larger landslide, with 457 of 531 electoral votes and 57.6% of the popular vote. The level of campaigning was curtailed out of health considerations.

Eisenhower valued the brief respites and the amenities of an office which he endowed with an arduous daily schedule. He made full use of his valet, chauffeur, and secretarial support—he rarely drove or dialed a phone number. He was an avid fisherman, golfer, painter, and bridge player, and preferred active rather than passive forms of entertainment. On August 26, 1959, Eisenhower was aboard the maiden flight of Air Force One, which replaced the previous Presidential aircraft, the *Columbine*.

Interstate Highway System

> Remarks in Cadillac Square, Detroit
> President Eisenhower delivered remarks about the need for a new highway program at Cadillac Square in Detroit on October 29, 1954
> Text of speech excerpt[32]

Problems playing this file? See media help.

Eisenhower was assured of an enduring achievement when he championed and signed the bill that authorized the Interstate Highway System in 1956. He justified the project through the Federal Aid Highway Act of 1956 as essential to American security during the Cold War. It was believed that large cities would be targets in a possible war, hence the highways were designed to facilitate their evacuation and ease military maneuvers.

Eisenhower's goal to create improved highways was influenced by difficulties encountered during his involvement in the U.S. Army's 1919 Transcontinental Motor Convoy. He was assigned as an observer for the mission, which involved sending a convoy of U.S. Army vehicles coast to coast. His subsequent experience with encountering German autobahn limited-access road systems during the concluding stages of World War II convinced him of the benefits of an Interstate Highway System. The Interstate Highway System could also be used as a runway for airplanes, which would be beneficial to war efforts. This system was put into place by Franklin D. Roosevelt, in 1944, under the Federal-Aid Highway Act of 1944. Noticing the improved ability to move logistics throughout the country, he thought an Interstate Highway System in the U.S. would not only be beneficial for military operations, but provide a measure of continued economic growth. The legislation initially stalled in the Congress over the issuance of bonds to finance the project, but the legislative effort was renewed and the law was signed by Eisenhower in June 1956.

Foreign policy

In 1953, the Republican Party's Old Guard presented Eisenhower with a dilemma by insisting he disavow the Yalta Agreements as beyond the constitutional authority of the Executive Branch; however, the death of Joseph Stalin in March 1953 made the matter a moot point. At this time Eisenhower gave his Chance for Peace speech in which he attempted, unsuccessfully, to forestall the nuclear arms race with the Soviet Union by suggesting multiple opportunities presented by peaceful uses of nuclear materials. Biographer Stephen Ambrose opined that this was the best speech of Eisenhower's presidency.[33]

Figure 19: *Eisenhower with Indian Prime Minister Jawaharlal Nehru*

Figure 20: *U.S. President Eisenhower visits the Republic of China and its President Chiang Kai-shek at Taipei.*

Figure 21: *Soviet Premier Nikita Khrushchev during his 11-day U.S. visit as guest of President Eisenhower, September 1959*

Nevertheless, the Cold War escalated during his presidency. When the Soviet Union successfully tested a hydrogen bomb in late November 1955, Eisenhower, against the advice of Dulles, decided to initiate a disarmament proposal to the Soviets. In an attempt to make their refusal more difficult, he proposed that both sides agree to dedicate fissionable material away from weapons toward peaceful uses, such as power generation. This approach was labeled "Atoms for Peace".

The U.N. speech was well received but the Soviets never acted upon it, due to an overarching concern for the greater stockpiles of nuclear weapons in the U.S. arsenal. Indeed, Eisenhower embarked upon a greater reliance on the use of nuclear weapons, while reducing conventional forces, and with them the overall defense budget, a policy formulated as a result of Project Solarium and expressed in NSC 162/2. This approach became known as the "New Look", and was initiated with defense cuts in late 1953.

In 1955 American nuclear arms policy became one aimed primarily at arms control as opposed to disarmament. The failure of negotiations over arms until 1955 was due mainly to the refusal of the Russians to permit any sort of inspections. In talks located in London that year, they expressed a willingness to discuss inspections; the tables were then turned on Eisenhower, when he responded with an unwillingness on the part of the U.S. to permit inspections. In May of that year the Russians agreed to sign a treaty giving independence to Austria, and paved the way for a Geneva summit with the U.S., U.K. and France. At the Geneva Conference Eisenhower presented a proposal called "Open Skies" to facilitate disarmament, which included plans for Russia and the U.S. to provide mutual access to each other's skies for open surveillance of military infrastructure. Russian leader Nikita Khrushchev dismissed the proposal out of hand.

In 1954, Eisenhower articulated the domino theory in his outlook towards communism in Southeast Asia and also in Central America. He believed that if the communists were allowed to prevail in Vietnam, this would cause a succession of countries to fall to communism, from Laos through Malaysia and Indonesia ultimately to India. Likewise, the fall of Guatemala would end with the fall of neighboring Mexico. That year the loss of North Vietnam to the communists and the rejection of his proposed European Defence Community (EDC) were serious defeats, but he remained optimistic in his opposition to the spread of communism, saying "Long faces don't win wars". As he had threatened the French in their rejection of EDC, he afterwards moved to restore West Germany, as a full NATO partner.

With Eisenhower's leadership and Dulles' direction, CIA activities increased under the pretense of resisting the spread of communism in poorer countries; the CIA in part deposed the leaders of Iran in Operation Ajax, of Guatemala through Operation Pbsuccess, and possibly the newly independent Republic of the Congo (Léopoldville). In 1954 Eisenhower wanted to increase surveillance inside the Soviet Union. With Dulles' recommendation, he authorized the deployment of thirty Lockheed U-2's at a cost of $35 million. The Eisenhower administration also planned the Bay of Pigs Invasion to overthrow Fidel Castro in Cuba, which John F. Kennedy was left to carry out.[34]

Space Race

Eisenhower and the CIA had known since at least January 1957, nine months before Sputnik, that Russia had the capability to launch a small payload into orbit and was likely to do so within a year.[35] He may also privately have welcomed the Russian satellite for its legal implications: By launching a satellite, Russia had in effect acknowledged that space was open to anyone who could access it, without needing permission from other nations.

On the whole, Eisenhower's support of the nation's fledgling space program was officially modest until the Soviet launch of Sputnik in 1957, gaining the Cold War enemy enormous prestige around the world. He then launched a

Figure 22: *President Eisenhower with Wernher von Braun, 1960*

national campaign that funded not just space exploration but a major strengthening of science and higher education. The Eisenhower administration determined to adopt a non-aggressive policy that would allow "space-crafts of any state to overfly all states, a region free of military posturing and launch Earth satellites to explore space".[36] His Open Skies Policy attempted to legitimize illegal Lockheed U-2 flyovers and Project Genetrix while paving the way for spy satellite technology to orbit over sovereign territory,[37] however Nikolai Bulganin and Nikita Khrushchev declined Eisenhower's proposal at the Geneva conference in July 1955.[38] In response to Sputnik being launched in October 1957, Eisenhower created NASA as a civilian space agency in October 1958, signed a landmark science education law, and improved relations with American scientists.[39]

Fear spread through the United States that the Soviet Union would invade and spread communism, so Eisenhower wanted to not only create a surveillance satellite to detect any threats but ballistic missiles that would protect the United States. In strategic terms, it was Eisenhower who devised the American basic strategy of nuclear deterrence based upon the triad of B-52 bombers, land-based intercontinental ballistic missiles (ICBMs), and Polaris submarine-launched ballistic missiles (SLBMs).[40]

NASA planners projected that human spaceflight would pull the United States ahead in the Space Race as well as accomplishing their long time goal, however,

Figure 23: *Eisenhower in Korea with General Chung Il-kwon, and Baik Seon-yup, 1952*

in 1960, an Ad Hoc Panel on Man-in-Space concluded that "man-in-space can not be justified" and was too costly.[41] Eisenhower later resented the space program and its gargantuan price tag—he was quoted as saying, "Anyone who would spend $40 billion in a race to the moon for national prestige is nuts."[42]

Korean War, Free China and Red China

In late 1952 Eisenhower went to Korea and discovered a military and political stalemate. Once in office, when the Chinese communists began a buildup in the Kaesong sanctuary, he threatened to use nuclear force if an armistice was not concluded. His earlier military reputation in Europe was effective with the Chinese communists. The National Security Council, the Joint Chiefs of Staff, and the Strategic Air Command (SAC) devised detailed plans for nuclear war against Red China. With the death of Stalin in early March 1953, Russian support for a Chinese communists hard-line weakened and Red China decided to compromise on the prisoner issue.[43]

In July 1953, an armistice took effect with Korea divided along approximately the same boundary as in 1950. The armistice and boundary remain in effect today. The armistice, concluded despite opposition from Secretary Dulles, South Korean President Syngman Rhee, and also within Eisenhower's party, has been described by biographer Ambrose as the greatest achievement of the administration. Eisenhower had the insight to realize that unlimited war in the nuclear age was unthinkable, and limited war unwinnable.

A point of emphasis in Ike's campaign had been his endorsement of a policy of liberation from communism as opposed to a policy of containment. This remained his preference despite the armistice with Korea. Throughout his terms Eisenhower took a hard-line attitude toward Red China, as demanded by conservative Republicans, with the goal of driving a wedge between Red China and the Soviet Union.

Eisenhower continued Truman's policy of recognizing the Republic of China (Free China) as the legitimate government of China, not the Beijing regime. There were localized flare-ups when the People's Liberation Army began shelling the islands of Quemoy and Matsu in September 1954. Eisenhower received recommendations embracing every variation of response to the aggression of the Chinese communists. He thought it essential to have every possible option available to him as the crisis unfolded.

The Sino-American Mutual Defense Treaty with the Republic of China was signed in December 1954. He requested and secured from Congress their "Free China Resolution" in January 1955, which gave Eisenhower unprecedented power in advance to use military force at any level of his choosing in defense of Free China and the Pescadores. The Resolution bolstered the morale of the Chinese nationalists, and signaled to Beijing that the U.S. was committed to holding the line.

Eisenhower openly threatened the Chinese communists with use of nuclear weapons, authorizing a series of bomb tests labeled Operation Teapot. Nevertheless, he left the Chinese communists guessing as to the exact nature of his nuclear response. This allowed Eisenhower to accomplish all of his objectives—the end of this communist encroachment, the retention of the Islands by the Chinese nationalists and continued peace. Defense of the Republic of China from an invasion remains a core American policy.

By the end of 1954 Eisenhower's military and foreign policy experts—the NSC, JCS and State Dept.—had unanimously urged him, on no less than five occasions, to launch an atomic attack against Red China; yet he consistently refused to do so and felt a distinct sense of accomplishment in having sufficiently confronted communism while keeping world peace.

The Middle East and Eisenhower doctrine

Even before he was inaugurated Eisenhower accepted a request from the British government to restore the Shah of Iran (Mohammad Reza Pahlavi) to power. He therefore authorized the Central Intelligence Agency to overthrow

Figure 24: *Eisenhower with the Shah of Iran, Mohammad Reza Pahlavi (1959)*

Prime Minister Mohammad Mosaddegh.[44] This resulted in an increased strategic control over Iranian oil by U.S. and British companies.

In November 1956, Eisenhower forced an end to the combined British, French and Israeli invasion of Egypt in response to the Suez Crisis, receiving praise from Egyptian president Gamal Abdel Nasser. Simultaneously he condemned the brutal Soviet invasion of Hungary in response to the Hungarian Revolution of 1956. He publicly disavowed his allies at the United Nations, and used financial and diplomatic pressure to make them withdraw from Egypt.[45] Eisenhower explicitly defended his strong position against Britain and France in his memoirs, which were published in 1965.[46]

After the Suez Crisis the United States became the protector of unstable friendly governments in the Middle East via the "Eisenhower Doctrine". Designed by Secretary of State Dulles, it held the U.S. would be "prepared to use armed force ... [to counter] aggression from any country controlled by international communism". Further, the United States would provide economic and military aid and, if necessary, use military force to stop the spread of communism in the Middle East.[47]

Eisenhower applied the doctrine in 1957–58 by dispensing economic aid to shore up the Kingdom of Jordan, and by encouraging Syria's neighbors to consider military operations against it. More dramatically, in July 1958, he

Figure 25: *Eisenhower and Vice President Richard Nixon with their host, King Saud of Saudi Arabia, at the Mayflower Hotel (1957)*

sent 15,000 Marines and soldiers to Lebanon as part of Operation Blue Bat, a non-combat peace-keeping mission to stabilize the pro-Western government and to prevent a radical revolution from sweeping over that country.

The mission proved a success and the Marines departed three months later. The deployment came in response to the urgent request of Lebanese president Camille Chamoun after sectarian violence had erupted in the country. Washington considered the military intervention successful since it brought about regional stability, weakened Soviet influence, and intimidated the Egyptian and Syrian governments, whose anti-West political position had hardened after the Suez Crisis.

Most Arab countries were skeptical about the "Eisenhower doctrine" because they considered "Zionist imperialism" the real danger. However, they did take the opportunity to obtain free money and weapons. Egypt and Syria, supported by the Soviet Union, openly opposed the initiative. However, Egypt received American aid until the Six-Day War in 1967.

As the Cold War deepened, Dulles sought to isolate the Soviet Union by building regional alliances of nations against it. Critics sometimes called it "pactomania".

Southeast Asia

Early in 1953, the French asked Eisenhower for help in French Indochina against the Communists, supplied from China, who were fighting the First Indochina War. Eisenhower sent Lt. General John W. "Iron Mike" O'Daniel to Vietnam to study and assess the French forces there.[48] Chief of Staff Matthew Ridgway dissuaded the President from intervening by presenting a comprehensive estimate of the massive military deployment that would be necessary. Eisenhower stated prophetically that "this war would absorb our troops by divisions."

Eisenhower did provide France with bombers and non-combat personnel. After a few months with no success by the French, he added other aircraft to drop napalm for clearing purposes. Further requests for assistance from the French were agreed to but only on conditions Eisenhower knew were impossible to meet – allied participation and congressional approval. When the French fortress of Dien Bien Phu fell to the Vietnamese Communists in May 1954, Eisenhower refused to intervene despite urgings from the Chairman of the Joint Chiefs, the Vice President and the head of NCS.

Eisenhower responded to the French defeat with the formation of the SEATO (Southeast Asia Treaty Organization) Alliance with the U.K., France, New Zealand and Australia in defense of Vietnam against communism. At that time the French and Chinese reconvened Geneva peace talks; Eisenhower agreed the U.S. would participate only as an observer. After France and the Communists agreed to a partition of Vietnam, Eisenhower rejected the agreement, offering military and economic aid to southern Vietnam.[49] Ambrose argues that Eisenhower, by not participating in the Geneva agreement, had kept the U.S. out of Vietnam; nevertheless, with the formation of SEATO, he had in the end put the U.S. back into the conflict.

In late 1954, Gen. J. Lawton Collins was made ambassador to "Free Vietnam" (the term South Vietnam came into use in 1955), effectively elevating the country to sovereign status. Collins' instructions were to support the leader Ngo Dinh Diem in subverting communism, by helping him to build an army and wage a military campaign. In February 1955, Eisenhower dispatched the first American soldiers to Vietnam as military advisors to Diem's army. After Diem announced the formation of the Republic of Vietnam (RVN, commonly known as South Vietnam) in October, Eisenhower immediately recognized the new state and offered military, economic, and technical assistance.

In the years that followed, Eisenhower increased the number of U.S. military advisors in South Vietnam to 900 men. This was due to North Vietnam's support of "uprisings" in the south and concern the nation would fall. In May 1957 Diem, then President of South Vietnam, made a state visit to the United

Figure 26: *A U-2 reconnaissance aircraft in flight*

States for ten days. President Eisenhower pledged his continued support, and a parade was held in Diem's honor in New York City. Although Diem was publicly praised, in private Secretary of State John Foster Dulles conceded that Diem had been selected because there were no better alternatives.[50]

After the election of November 1960, Eisenhower in briefing with John F. Kennedy pointed out the communist threat in Southeast Asia as requiring prioritization in the next administration. Eisenhower told Kennedy he considered Laos "the cork in the bottle" with regard to the regional threat.[51]

1960 U-2 incident

On May 1, 1960, a U.S. one-man U-2 spy plane was reportedly shot down at high altitude over Soviet Union airspace. The flight was made to gain photo intelligence before the scheduled opening of an East-West summit conference, which had been scheduled in Paris, 15 days later. Captain Francis Gary Powers had bailed out of his aircraft and was captured after parachuting down onto Russian soil. Four days after Powers disappeared, the Eisenhower Administration had NASA issue a very detailed press release noting that an aircraft had "gone missing" north of Turkey. It speculated that the pilot might have fallen unconscious while the autopilot was still engaged, and falsely claimed that "the pilot reported over the emergency frequency that he was experiencing oxygen difficulties."

Soviet Premier Nikita Khrushchev announced that a "spy-plane" had been shot down but intentionally made no reference to the pilot. As a result, the Eisenhower Administration, thinking the pilot had died in the crash, authorized the release of a cover story claiming that the plane was a "weather research aircraft" which had unintentionally strayed into Soviet airspace after the pilot had radioed "difficulties with his oxygen equipment" while flying over Turkey. The Soviets put Captain Powers on trial and displayed parts of the U-2, which had been recovered almost fully intact.[52]

The 1960 Four Power Paris Summit with Eisenhower, Nikita Khrushchev, Harold Macmillan and Charles de Gaulle collapsed because of the incident. Eisenhower refused to accede to Khrushchev's demands that he apologize. Therefore, Khrushchev would not take part in the summit. Up until this event, Eisenhower felt he had been making progress towards better relations with the Soviet Union. Nuclear arms reduction and Berlin were to have been discussed at the summit. Eisenhower stated it had all been ruined because of that "stupid U-2 business".

The affair was an embarrassment for United States prestige. Further, the Senate Foreign Relations Committee held a lengthy inquiry into the U-2 incident. In Russia, Captain Powers made a forced confession and apology. On August 19, 1960, Powers was convicted of espionage and sentenced to imprisonment. On February 10, 1962, Powers was exchanged for Rudolf Abel in Berlin and returned to the U.S.

Civil rights

While President Truman had begun the process of desegregating the Armed Forces in 1948, actual implementation had been slow. Eisenhower made clear his stance in his first State of the Union address in February 1953, saying "I propose to use whatever authority exists in the office of the President to end segregation in the District of Columbia, including the Federal Government, and any segregation in the Armed Forces".[53] When he encountered opposition from the services, he used government control of military spending to force the change through, stating "Wherever Federal Funds are expended ..., I do not see how any American can justify ... a discrimination in the expenditure of those funds".

When Robert B. Anderson, Eisenhower's first Secretary of the Navy, argued that the U.S. Navy must recognize the "customs and usages prevailing in certain geographic areas of our country which the Navy had no part in creating," Eisenhower overruled him: "We have not taken and we shall not take a single backward step. There must be no second class citizens in this country."[54]

The administration declared racial discrimination a national security issue, as Communists around the world used the racial discrimination and history of violence in the U.S. as a point of propaganda attack.[55]

Eisenhower told District of Columbia officials to make Washington a model for the rest of the country in integrating black and white public school children. He proposed to Congress the Civil Rights Act of 1957 and of 1960 and signed those acts into law. The 1957 act for the first time established a permanent civil rights office inside the Justice Department and a Civil Rights Commission to hear testimony about abuses of voting rights. Although both acts were much weaker than subsequent civil rights legislation, they constituted the first significant civil rights acts since 1875.

In 1957, the state of Arkansas refused to honor a federal court order to integrate their public school system stemming from the *Brown* decision. Eisenhower demanded that Arkansas governor Orval Faubus obey the court order. When Faubus balked, the president placed the Arkansas National Guard under federal control and sent in the 101st Airborne Division. They escorted and protected nine black students' entry to Little Rock Central High School, an all-white public school, for the first time since the Reconstruction Era. Martin Luther King Jr. wrote to Eisenhower to thank him for his actions, writing "The overwhelming majority of southerners, Negro and white, stand firmly behind your resolute action to restore law and order in Little Rock".[56]

Eisenhower's administration contributed to the McCarthyist Lavender Scare with President Eisenhower issuing his Executive Order 10450 in 1953. During Eisenhower's presidency thousands of lesbian and gay applicants were barred from federal employment and over 5,000 federal employees were fired under suspicions of being homosexual. From 1947 to 1961 the number of firings based on sexual orientation were far greater than those for membership in the Communist party, and government officials intentionally campaigned to make "homosexual" synonymous with "Communist traitor" such that LGBT people were treated as a national security threat stemming from the belief they were susceptible to blackmail and exploitation.

Relations with Congress

Eisenhower had a Republican Congress for only his first two years in office; in the Senate, the Republican majority was by a one-vote margin. Senator Robert A. Taft assisted the President greatly in working with the Old Guard, and was sorely missed when his death (in July 1953) left Eisenhower with his successor William Knowland, whom Eisenhower disliked.

This prevented Eisenhower from openly condemning Joseph McCarthy's highly criticized methods against communism. To facilitate relations with

Congress, Eisenhower decided to ignore McCarthy's controversies and thereby deprive them of more energy from involvement of the White House. This position drew criticism from a number of corners. In late 1953, McCarthy declared on national television that the employment of communists within the government was a menace and would be a pivotal issue in the 1954 Senate elections. Eisenhower was urged to respond directly and specify the various measures he had taken to purge the government of communists.

Among Eisenhower's objectives in not directly confronting McCarthy was to prevent McCarthy from dragging the Atomic Energy Commission (AEC) into McCarthy's witch hunt for communists, which would interfere with, and perhaps delay, the AEC's important work on H-bombs. The administration had discovered through its own investigations that one of the leading scientists on the AEC, J. Robert Oppenheimer, had urged that the H-bomb work be delayed. Eisenhower removed him from the agency and revoked his security clearance, though he knew this would create fertile ground for McCarthy.

In May 1955, McCarthy threatened to issue subpoenas to White House personnel. Eisenhower was furious, and issued an order as follows: "It is essential to efficient and effective administration that employees of the Executive Branch be in a position to be completely candid in advising with each other on official matters ... it is not in the public interest that any of their conversations or communications, or any documents or reproductions, concerning such advice be disclosed." This was an unprecedented step by Eisenhower to protect communication beyond the confines of a cabinet meeting, and soon became a tradition known as executive privilege. Ike's denial of McCarthy's access to his staff reduced McCarthy's hearings to rants about trivial matters, and contributed to his ultimate downfall.

In early 1954, the Old Guard put forward a constitutional amendment, called the Bricker Amendment, which would curtail international agreements by the Chief Executive, such as the Yalta Agreements. Eisenhower opposed the measure. The Old Guard agreed with Eisenhower on the development and ownership of nuclear reactors by private enterprises, which the Democrats opposed. The President succeeded in getting legislation creating a system of licensure for nuclear plants by the AEC.

The Democrats gained a majority in both houses in the 1954 election. Eisenhower had to work with the Democratic Majority Leader Lyndon B. Johnson (later U.S. president) in the Senate and Speaker Sam Rayburn in the House, both from Texas. Joe Martin, the Republican Speaker from 1947 to 1949 and again from 1953 to 1955, wrote that Eisenhower "never surrounded himself with assistants who could solve political problems with professional skill. There were exceptions, Leonard W. Hall, for example, who as chairman of the Republican National Committee tried to open the administration's eyes to the political facts of life, with occasional success. However, these exceptions were not enough to right the balance."[57]

Speaker Martin concluded that Eisenhower worked too much through subordinates in dealing with Congress, with results, "often the reverse of what he has desired" because Members of Congress, "resent having some young fellow who was picked up by the White House without ever having been elected to office himself coming around and telling them 'The Chief wants this'. The administration never made use of many Republicans of consequence whose services in one form or another would have been available for the asking."

Judicial appointments

Supreme Court

Eisenhower appointed the following Justices to the Supreme Court of the United States:

- Earl Warren, 1953 (Chief Justice)
- John Marshall Harlan II, 1954
- William J. Brennan, 1956
- Charles Evans Whittaker, 1957
- Potter Stewart, 1958

Whittaker was unsuited for the role and soon retired. Stewart and Harlan were conservative Republicans, while Brennan was a Democrat who became a leading voice for liberalism.[58] In selecting a Chief Justice, Eisenhower looked for an experienced jurist who could appeal to liberals in the party as well as law-and-order conservatives, noting privately that Warren "represents the kind of political, economic, and social thinking that I believe we need on the Supreme Court ... He has a national name for integrity, uprightness, and courage that, again, I believe we need on the Court". In the next few years Warren led the Court in a series of liberal decisions that revolutionized the role of the Court.

States admitted to the Union

- Alaska – January 3, 1959 49th state
- Hawaii – August 21, 1959 50th state

Health issues

Eisenhower began chain smoking cigarettes at West Point, often three or four packs a day. He joked that he "gave [himself] an order" to stop cold turkey in 1949. But Evan Thomas says the true story was more complex. At first he removed cigarettes and ashtrays, but that did not work. He told a friend:

> I decided to make a game of the whole business and try to achieve a feeling of some superiority ... So I stuffed cigarettes in every pocket, put them around my office on the desk ... [and] made it a practice to offer a cigarette to anyone who came in ... while mentally reminding myself as I sat down, "I do not have to do what that poor fellow is doing."

He was the first president to release information about his health and medical records while in office, but people around him deliberately misled the public about his health. On September 24, 1955, while vacationing in Colorado, he had a serious heart attack.[59] Dr. Howard Snyder, his personal physician, misdiagnosed the symptoms as indigestion, and failed to call in the help that was urgently needed. Snyder later falsified his own records to cover his blunder and to protect Eisenhower's need to portray he was healthy enough to do his job.[60,61,62]

The heart attack required six weeks' hospitalization, during which time Nixon, Dulles, and Sherman Adams assumed administrative duties and provided communication with the President. He was treated by Dr. Paul Dudley White, a cardiologist with a national reputation, who regularly informed the press of the President's progress. Instead of eliminating him as a candidate for a second term as President, his physician recommended a second term as essential to his recovery.

As a consequence of his heart attack, Eisenhower developed a left ventricular aneurysm, which was in turn the cause of a mild stroke on November 25, 1957. This incident occurred during a cabinet meeting when Eisenhower suddenly found himself unable to speak or move his right hand. The stroke had caused an aphasia. The president also suffered from Crohn's disease, chronic inflammatory condition of the intestine, which necessitated surgery for a bowel obstruction on June 9, 1956. To treat the intestinal block, surgeons bypassed about ten inches of his small intestine. His scheduled meeting with Indian Prime Minister Jawaharlal Nehru was postponed so he could recover at his farm. He was still recovering from this operation during the Suez Crisis. Eisenhower's health issues forced him to give up smoking and make some changes to his dietary habits, but he still indulged in alcohol. During a visit to England he complained of dizziness and had to have his blood pressure checked on August 29, 1959; however, before dinner at Chequers on the next day his doctor General Howard Snyder recalled Eisenhower "drank several

Figure 27: *The official White House portrait of Dwight D. Eisenhower*

gin-and-tonics, and one or two gins on the rocks ... three or four wines with the dinner".[63]

The last three years of Eisenhower's second term in office were ones of relatively good health. Eventually after leaving the White House, he suffered several additional and ultimately crippling heart attacks. A severe heart attack in August 1965 largely ended his participation in public affairs. In August 1966 he began to show symptoms of cholecystitis, for which he underwent surgery on December 12, 1966, when his gallbladder was removed, containing 16 gallstones. After Eisenhower's death in 1969 (see below), an autopsy unexpectedly revealed an adrenal pheochromocytoma,[64] a benign adrenaline-secreting tumor that may have made the President more vulnerable to heart disease. Eisenhower suffered seven heart attacks from 1955 until his death.

End of presidency

The 22nd Amendment to the U.S. Constitution was ratified in 1951, and it set term limits to the presidency of two terms. Truman as the incumbent was not covered. Eisenhower became the first U.S. president constitutionally prevented from running for re-election to a third term.

Eisenhower was also the first outgoing President to come under the protection of the Former Presidents Act; two living former Presidents, Herbert Hoover and Harry S. Truman, left office before the Act was passed. Under the act, Eisenhower was entitled to receive a lifetime pension, state-provided staff and a Secret Service detail.

In the 1960 election to choose his successor, Eisenhower endorsed Nixon over Democrat John F. Kennedy. He told friends, "I will do almost anything to avoid turning my chair and country over to Kennedy." He actively campaigned for Nixon in the final days, although he may have done Nixon some harm. When asked by reporters at the end of a televised press conference to list one of Nixon's policy ideas he had adopted, Eisenhower joked, "If you give me a week, I might think of one. I don't remember." Kennedy's campaign used the quote in one of its campaign commercials. Nixon narrowly lost to Kennedy. Eisenhower, who was the oldest president in history at that time (then 70), was succeeded by the youngest elected president, as Kennedy was 43.

It was originally intended for President Eisenhower to have a more active role in the campaign as he wanted to respond to attacks Kennedy made on his administration. However, First Lady Mamie Eisenhower expressed concern to Second Lady Pat Nixon about the strain campaigning would put on his heart and wanted the President to back out of it without letting him know of her intervention. Vice President Nixon himself also received concern from White House physician Major General Howard Snyder, who informed him that he could not approve a heavy campaign schedule for the President and his health had been exacerbated by Kennedy's attacks. Nixon then convinced Eisenhower not to go ahead with the expanded campaign schedule and limit himself to the original schedule. Nixon reflected that if Eisenhower had carried out his expanded campaign schedule he might have had a decisive impact on the outcome of the election, especially in states that Kennedy won with razor-thin margins. It was years later before Mamie told Dwight why Nixon changed his mind on Dwight's campaigning.[65]

On January 17, 1961, Eisenhower gave his final televised Address to the Nation from the Oval Office. In his farewell speech, Eisenhower raised the issue of the Cold War and role of the U.S. armed forces. He described the Cold War: "We face a hostile ideology global in scope, atheistic in character, ruthless in purpose and insidious in method ..." and warned about what he saw as unjustified government spending proposals and continued with a warning that "we must guard against the acquisition of unwarranted influence, whether sought or unsought, by the military–industrial complex."

He elaborated, "we recognize the imperative need for this development ... the potential for the disastrous rise of misplaced power exists and will persist ... Only an alert and knowledgeable citizenry can compel the proper meshing of the huge industrial and military machinery of defense with our peaceful methods and goals, so that security and liberty may prosper together."

Figure 28: *Eisenhower speaks to the press at the 1964 Republican National Convention*

Because of legal issues related to holding a military rank while in a civilian office, Eisenhower had resigned his permanent commission as General of the Army before entering the office of President of the United States. Upon completion of his Presidential term, his commission was reactivated by Congress and Eisenhower again was commissioned a five-star general in the United States Army.[66]

Post-presidency, death and funeral

Following the presidency, Eisenhower moved to the place where he and Mamie had spent much of their post-war time. The home was a working farm adjacent to the battlefield at Gettysburg, Pennsylvania, 70 miles from his ancestral home in Elizabethville, Dauphin County, Pennsylvania. They also maintained a retirement home in Palm Desert, California. In 1967 the Eisenhowers donated the Gettysburg farm to the National Park Service.

After leaving office, Eisenhower did not completely retreat from political life. He flew to San Antonio, where he had been stationed years earlier, to support John W. Goode, the unsuccessful Republican candidate against the Democrat Henry B. Gonzalez for Texas' 20th congressional district seat. He addressed the 1964 Republican National Convention, in San Francisco, and appeared

Figure 29: *President Lyndon Johnson with Eisenhower aboard Air Force One in October 1965*

Figure 30: *Eisenhower's funeral service*

Figure 31: *Graves of Dwight D. Eisenhower, Doud Dwight "Icky" Eisenhower and Mamie Eisenhower in Abilene, Kansas*

with party nominee Barry Goldwater in a campaign commercial from his Gettysburg retreat. That endorsement came somewhat reluctantly because Goldwater had in the late 1950s criticized Eisenhower's administration as "a dimestore New Deal". On January 20, 1969, the day Nixon was inaugurated as President, Eisenhower issued a statement praising his former vice president and calling it a "day for rejoicing".

On the morning of March 28, 1969, Eisenhower died in Washington, D.C., of congestive heart failure at Walter Reed Army Medical Center; he was 78 years old. The following day, his body was moved to the Washington National Cathedral's Bethlehem Chapel, where he lay in repose for 28 hours. On March 30, his body was brought by caisson to the United States Capitol, where he lay in state in the Capitol Rotunda. On March 31, Eisenhower's body was returned to the National Cathedral, where he was given an Episcopal Church funeral service.

That evening, Eisenhower's body was placed onto a special train for its journey from the nation's capital to Abilene, Kansas. This was the last time a funeral train has been used as part of funeral proceedings for an American president.WP:NOTRS His body arrived on April 2, and was interred that day in a small chapel on the grounds of the Eisenhower Presidential Library. The president's body was buried as a General of the Army. The family used an $80 standard soldier's casket, and dressed his body in his famous short green jacket. The medals worn were: the Army Distinguished Service Medal with three oak leaf clusters, the Navy Distinguished Service Medal, and the Legion of Merit. Eisenhower is buried alongside his son Doud, who died at age 3 in 1921. His wife Mamie was buried next to him after her death a decade later in 1979.

President Richard Nixon eulogized Eisenhower, saying:

> *Some men are considered great because they lead great armies or they lead powerful nations. For eight years now, Dwight Eisenhower has neither commanded an army nor led a nation; and yet he remained through his final days the world's most admired and respected man, truly the first citizen of the world.*

Legacy and memory

Eisenhower's reputation declined in the immediate years after he left office. During his presidency, he was widely seen by critics as an inactive, uninspiring, golf-playing president. This was in stark contrast to his vigorous young successor, John F. Kennedy, who was 26 years his junior. Despite his unprecedented use of Army troops to enforce a federal desegregation order at Central High School in Little Rock, Eisenhower was criticized for his reluctance to support the civil rights movement to the degree that activists wanted. Eisenhower also attracted criticism for his handling of the 1960 U-2 incident and the associated international embarrassment, for the Soviet Union's perceived leadership in the nuclear arms race and the Space Race, and for his failure to publicly oppose McCarthyism.

In particular, Eisenhower was criticized for failing to defend George Marshall from attacks by Joseph McCarthy, though he privately deplored McCarthy's tactics and claims.

Historian John Lewis Gaddis has summarized a more recent turnaround in evaluations by historians:

> *Historians long ago abandoned the view that Eisenhower's was a failed presidency. He did, after all, end the Korean War without getting into any others. He stabilized, and did not escalate, the Soviet–American rivalry. He strengthened European alliances while withdrawing support from European colonialism. He rescued the Republican Party from isolationism and McCarthyism. He maintained prosperity, balanced the budget, promoted technological innovation, facilitated (if reluctantly) the civil rights movement and warned, in the most memorable farewell address since Washington's, of a "military–industrial complex" that could endanger the nation's liberties. Not until Reagan would another president leave*

Figure 32: *Eisenhower signs the legislation that changes Armistice Day to Veterans Day, June 1, 1954.*

office with so strong a sense of having accomplished what he set out to do.[67]

Although conservatism in politics was strong during the 1950s and Eisenhower generally espoused conservative sentiments, his administration concerned itself mostly with foreign affairs (an area in which the career-military president had more knowledge) and pursued a hands-off domestic policy. Eisenhower looked to moderation and cooperation as a means of governance.

Although he sought to slow or contain the New Deal and other federal programs, he did not attempt to repeal them outright, and in doing so was popular among the liberal wing of the Republican Party. Conservative critics of his administration found that he did not do enough to advance the goals of the right; according to Hans Morgenthau, "Eisenhower's victories were but accidents without consequence in the history of the Republican party."[68]

Since the 19th century, many if not all presidents were assisted by a central figure or "gatekeeper", sometimes described as the president's private secretary, sometimes with no official title at all. Eisenhower formalized this role, introducing the office of White House Chief of Staff – an idea he borrowed from the United States Army. Every president after Lyndon Johnson has also

Figure 33: *President John F. Kennedy meets with Eisenhower at Camp David, April 22, 1961, three days after the failed Bay of Pigs Invasion.*

appointed staff to this position. Initially, Gerald Ford and Jimmy Carter tried to operate without a chief of staff, but each eventually appointed one.

As president, Eisenhower also initiated the "up or out" policy that still prevails in the U.S. military, whereby officers who are passed over for promotion twice are usually honorably but quickly discharged to make way for younger, more able officers. (As an army officer, Eisenhower had been stuck at the rank of major for 16 years between the two world wars.)

On December 20, 1944, Eisenhower was appointed to the rank of General of the Army, placing him in the company of George Marshall, Henry "Hap" Arnold, and Douglas MacArthur, the only four men to achieve the rank in World War Two, and along with Omar Bradley, one of only five men to achieve the rank since the August 5, 1888 death of Philip Sheridan, and the only five men to hold the rank as a Five-star general. The rank was created by an Act of Congress on a temporary basis when Public Law 78-482 was passed on December 14, 1944,[69] as a temporary rank, subject to reversion to permanent rank six months after the end of the war. The temporary rank was then declared permanent March 23, 1946 by Public Law 333 of the 79th Congress, which also awarded full pay and allowances in the grade to those on the retired list.[70] It was created to give the most senior American commanders parity of rank with their British counterparts holding the ranks of field marshal and admiral of the fleet. This second General of the Army rank is not the same as the post-Civil War era version because of its purpose and five stars.

Eisenhower founded People to People International in 1956, based on his belief that citizen interaction would promote cultural interaction and world peace. The program includes a student ambassador component, which sends American youth on educational trips to other countries.

Frank Gasparro's obverse design (left) and reverse design (right) of the Presidential Medal of Appreciation award during Eisenhower's official visit to the State of Hawaii from June 20–25, 1960.

During his second term as president, Eisenhower distinctively preserved his presidential gratitude by awarding individuals a special memento. This memento was a series of specially designed U.S. Mint presidential appreciation medals. Eisenhower presented the medal as an expression of his appreciation and the medal is a keepsake reminder for the recipient.

The development of the appreciation medals was initiated by the White House and executed by the Bureau of the Mint through the U.S. Mint in Philadelphia. The medals were struck from September 1958 through October 1960. A total of twenty designs are cataloged with a total mintage of 9,858. Each of the designs incorporates the text "with appreciation" or "with personal and official gratitude" accompanied with Eisenhower's initials "D.D.E." or facsimile signature. The design also incorporates location, date, and/or significant event. Prior to the end of his second term as President, 1,451 medals were turned in to the Bureau of the Mint and destroyed. The Eisenhower appreciation medals are part of the Presidential Medal of Appreciation Award Medal Series.

Figure 34: *Eisenhower Interstate System sign south of San Antonio, Texas*

Tributes and memorials

The Interstate Highway System is officially known as the "Dwight D. Eisenhower National System of Interstate and Defense Highways" in his honor. It was inspired in part by Eisenhower's own Army experiences in World War II, where he recognized the advantages of the autobahn system in Germany. Commemorative signs reading "Eisenhower Interstate System" and bearing Eisenhower's permanent 5-star rank insignia were introduced in 1993 and now are displayed throughout the Interstate System. Several highways are also named for him, including the Eisenhower Expressway (Interstate 290) near Chicago. the Eisenhower Tunnel on Interstate 70 west of Denver, and Interstate 80 in California.

Dwight D. Eisenhower School for National Security and Resource Strategy is a senior war college of the Department of Defense's National Defense University in Washington, DC. Eisenhower graduated from this school when it was previously known as the Army Industrial College. The school's building on Fort Lesley J. McNair, when it was known as the Industrial College of the Armed Forces, was dedicated as Eisenhower Hall in 1960.

Eisenhower was honored on a US one dollar coin, minted from 1971 to 1978. His centenary was honored on a commemorative dollar coin issued in 1990.

Figure 35: *Bronze statue of Eisenhower at Capitol rotunda*

In 1969, four major record companies – ABC Records, MGM Records, Buddha Records and Caedmon Audio – released tribute albums in Eisenhower's honor.

In 1999, the United States Congress created the Dwight D. Eisenhower Memorial Commission, to create an enduring national memorial in Washington, D.C.. In 2009, the commission chose the architect Frank Gehry to design the memorial. The memorial will stand on a four-acre site near the National Mall on Maryland Avenue, SW across the street from the National Air and Space Museum.

Awards and decorations

U.S. Military Decorations	
	Army Distinguished Service Medal w/ 4 oak leaf clusters
	Navy Distinguished Service Medal
	Legion of Merit
U.S. Service Medals	
	Mexican Border Service Medal

	World War I Victory Medal
	American Defense Service Medal
	European-African-Middle Eastern Campaign Medal w/ 9 campaign stars
	World War II Victory Medal
	Army of Occupation Medal w/ "Germany" clasp
	National Defense Service Medal w/ 1 service star
International and Foreign Awards	
	Order of the Liberator San Martin, Grand Cross (Argentina)
	Grand Decoration of Honour in Gold with Sash (Austria)
	Order of Leopold, Grand Cordon (Belgium)
	Croix de guerre w/ palm (Belgium)
	Order of the Southern Cross, Grand Cross (Brazil)
	Order of Military Merit (Brazil), Grand Cross
	Order of Aeronautical Merit, Grand Cross (Brazil)
	War Medal (Brazil)
	Campaign Medal (Brazil)
	Order of Merit, Grand Cross (Chile)
	Order of the Cloud and Banner, with Special Grand Cordon, (China)
	Military Order of the White Lion, Grand Cross (Czechoslovakia)
	War Cross 1939–1945 (Czechoslovakia)
	Order of the Elephant, Knight (Denmark)
	Order of Abdon Calderón, First Class (Ecuador)
	Order of Ismail, Grand Cordon (Egypt)
	Order of Solomon, Knight Grand Cross with Cordon (Ethiopia)
	Order of the Queen of Sheba, Member (Ethiopia)
	Legion of Honor, Grand Cross (France)
	Order of Liberation, Companion (France)
	Military Medal (France)
	Croix de guerre w/ palm (France)
	Royal Order of George I, Knight Grand Cross with Swords (Greece)
	Order of the Redeemer, Knight Grand Cross (Greece)
	Cross of Military Merit, First Class (Guatemala)
	National Order of Honour and Merit, Grand Cross with Gold Badge (Haiti)
	Order of the Holy Sepulchre, Knight Grand Cross (Holy See)

	Military Order of Italy, Knight Grand Cross with Swords (Italy)
	Order of the Chrysanthemum, Collar (Japan)
	Order of the Oak Crown, Grand Cross (Luxembourg)
	Military Medal (Luxembourg)
	Order pro merito Melitensi, KGC (Sovereign Military Order of Malta)
	Order of the Aztec Eagle, Collar (Mexico)
	Medal of Military Merit (Mexico)
No Ribbon	Medal of Civic Merit (Mexico)
	Order of Ouissam Alaouite, Grand Cross (Morocco)
	Order of the Netherlands Lion, Knight Grand Cross (Netherlands)
	Royal Norwegian Order of St. Olav, Grand Cross (Norway)
	Order of Nishan-e-Pakistan, First Class (Pakistan)
	Order of Manuel Amador Guerrero, Grand Officer (Panama)
	Orden Vasco Núñez de Balboa, Grand Cross (Panama)
	Order of Sikatuna, Grand Collar (Philippines)
	Legion of Honor (Philippines), Chief Commander (Philippines)
	Distinguished Service Star, (Philippines)
	Order of Polonia Restituta, Grand Cross (Poland)
	Order of Virtuti Militari, First Class (Poland)
	Cross of Grunwald, First Class (Poland)
	Order of the Royal House of Chakri, Knight (Thailand)
	Order of Glory, Grand Cordon (Tunisia)
	Order of the Bath, Knight Grand Cross (United Kingdom)
	Order of Merit, Member (United Kingdom)
	Africa Star, with "8" and "1" numerical devices (United Kingdom)
	Order of Victory, Star (USSR)
	Order of Suvorov, First Class (USSR)
	The Royal Yugoslav Commemorative War Cross (Yugoslavia)

Other honors

- An apartment at the top of the Culzean Castle in Scotland was given to General of the Army Dwight D. Eisenhower in recognition of his role as Supreme Commander of the Allied Forces in Europe during the Second World War. The General first visited Culzean Castle in 1946 and stayed there four times, including once while President of the United States. An

Figure 36: *The star of the Soviet Order of Victory awarded to Eisenhower*[71]

Figure 37: *The coat of arms granted to Eisenhower upon his incorporation as a knight of the Order of the Elephant in 1950. The anvil represents the fact that his name is derived from the German for "iron hewer".*

Eisenhower exhibition occupies one of the rooms, with mementos of his lifetime.
- In June 1945, Eisenhower received an honorary Freedom of the City of London.
- In January 1946, The Metropolitan Museum of Art named Eisenhower an Honorary Fellow for Life in recognition of his efforts to recover art looted by the Nazis during World War II.[72]
- In 1965, Eisenhower received an honorary doctorate from Grinnell College in Grinnell, Iowa.
- In 1966, Eisenhower was the second person awarded Civitan International's World Citizenship Award.
- In May 1967, Eisenhower was made an honorary brother of Epsilon Eta Chapter of Tau Epsilon Phi Fraternity.
- In December 1999, he was listed on Gallup's List of Most Widely Admired People of the 20th century.
- In 2009, he was named to the World Golf Hall of Fame in the Lifetime Achievement category for his contributions to the sport.

Promotions

No insignia	Cadet, United States Military Academy: June 14, 1911
No pin insignia in 1915	Second Lieutenant, Regular Army: June 12, 1915
	First Lieutenant, Regular Army: July 1, 1916
	Captain, Regular Army: May 15, 1917
	Major, National Army: June 17, 1918
	Lieutenant Colonel, National Army: October 20, 1918
	Captain, Regular Army: June 30, 1920 (Reverted to permanent rank.)
	Major, Regular Army: July 2, 1920
	Captain, Regular Army: November 4, 1922 (Discharged as major and appointed as captain due to reduction of Army.)
	Major, Regular Army: August 26, 1924

	Lieutenant Colonel, Regular Army: July 1, 1936
	Colonel, Army of the United States: March 6, 1941
	Brigadier General, Army of the United States: September 29, 1941
	Major General, Army of the United States: March 27, 1942
	Lieutenant General, Army of the United States: July 7, 1942
	General, Army of the United States: February 11, 1943
	Brigadier General, Regular Army: August 30, 1943
	Major General, Regular Army: August 30, 1943
	General of the Army, Army of the United States: December 20, 1944
	General of the Army, Regular Army: April 11, 1946

Note – Eisenhower relinquished his active duty status when he became president on January 20, 1953. He was returned to active duty when he left office eight years later.

Family tree

Bibliography

General biographies

<templatestyles src="Template:Refbegin/styles.css" />

- Ambrose, Stephen (1983). *Eisenhower: Soldier, General of the Army, President-Elect (1893–1952)*. **I**. New York: Simon & Schuster.
- Ambrose, Stephen (1984). *Eisenhower: The President (1952–1969)*. **II**. New York: Simon & Schuster.
- Boyle, Peter G. (2005). *Eisenhower*. Pearson/Longman. ISBN 0582287200. OCLC 55665502[73].
- D'Este, Carlo (2002). *Eisenhower: A Soldier's Life*. ISBN 0805056866.

- Krieg, Joann P. ed. (1987). *Dwight D. Eisenhower, Soldier, President, Statesman*. 24 essays by scholars. ISBN 0313259550
- Newton, Jim (2011). *Eisenhower: The White House Years*. Doubleday. ISBN 978-0-385-52353-0.
- Parmet, Herbert S. (1972). *Eisenhower and the American Crusades*. OCLC 482017[74].
- Smith, Jean Edward (2012). *Eisenhower in War and Peace*. Random House. ISBN 140006693X.
- Wicker, Tom (2002). *Dwight D. Eisenhower*. Times Books. ISBN 0805069070. OCLC 49893871[75].

Military career

- Ambrose, Stephen E. (1970) *The Supreme Commander: The War Years of Dwight D. Eisenhower* excerpt and text search[76]
- Ambrose, Stephen E. (1998). *The Victors: Eisenhower and his Boys: The Men of World War II*[77], New York : Simon & Schuster. ISBN 068485628X
- Eisenhower, David (1986). *Eisenhower at War 1943–1945*, New York : Random House. ISBN 0394412370. A detailed study by his grandson.
- Eisenhower, John S. D. (2003). *General Ike*, Free Press, New York. ISBN 0743244745
- Hobbs, Joseph Patrick (1999). *Dear General: Eisenhower's Wartime Letters to Marshall*. Baltimore: Johns Hopkins University Press. ISBN 0801862191.
- Irish, Kerry E. "Apt Pupil: Dwight Eisenhower and the 1930 Industrial Mobilization Plan", *The Journal of Military History* 70.1 (2006) 31–61 online in Project Muse.
- Jordan, Jonathan W. (2011). *Brothers Rivals Victors: Eisenhower, Patton, Bradley, and the Partnership that Drove the Allied Conquest in Europe*. NAL/Caliber. ISBN 0451232127. OCLC 617565184[78].
- Jordan, Jonathan W. (2015). *American Warlords: How Roosevelt's High Command Led America to Victory in World War II*. NAL/Caliber. ISBN 978-0451414571. OCLC 892458610[79].
- Pogue, Forrest C. (1954). *The Supreme Command*. Office of the Chief of Military History, Dept. of the Army. OCLC 1247005[80].
- Weigley, Russell (1981). *Eisenhower's Lieutenants: the Campaign of France and Germany, 1944–1945*. Indiana University Press. ISBN 0253133335. OCLC 6863111[81].

Civilian career

- Bowie, Robert R. and Immerman, Richard H. (1998). *Waging Peace: How Eisenhower Shaped an Enduring Cold War Strategy*, Oxford University Press. ISBN 0195062647
- Chernus, Ira (2008). *Apocalypse Management: Eisenhower and the Discourse of National Insecurity*. Stanford University Press. ISBN 978-0804758079. OCLC 105454244[82].
- Damms, Richard V. (2002). *The Eisenhower Presidency, 1953–1961*
- David Paul T., ed. (1954). *Presidential Nominating Politics in 1952*. 5 vols., Johns Hopkins Press. OCLC 519846[83]
- Divine, Robert A. (1981). *Eisenhower and the Cold War*.
- Gellman, Irwin F. (2015). *The President and the Apprentice: Eisenhower and Nixon, 1952–1961*. New Haven, CT: Yale University Press. ISBN 978-0300181050 OCLC 910504324[84]
- Greenstein, Fred I. (1991). *The Hidden-Hand Presidency: Eisenhower as Leader*. Basic Books. ISBN 0465029485 OCLC 8765635[85]
- Harris, Douglas B. "Dwight Eisenhower and the New Deal: The Politics of Preemption", *Presidential Studies Quarterly*, Vol. 27, 1997.
- Harris, Seymour E. (1962). *The Economics of the Political Parties, with Special Attention to Presidents Eisenhower and Kennedy*. OCLC 174566[86]
- Lasby, Clarence G. *Eisenhower's Heart Attack: How Ike Beat Heart Disease and Held on to the Presidency* (1997)
- Medhurst, Martin J. (1993). *Dwight D. Eisenhower: Strategic Communicator*. Westport, CT: Greenwood Press. ISBN 0313261407 OCLC 26764309[87]
- Mayer, Michael S. (2009). *The Eisenhower Years* Facts on File. ISBN 0816053871
- Newton, Jim. (2011) *Eisenhower: The White House Years* ISBN 978-0385523530 OCLC 694394274[88]
- Pach, Chester J., and Richardson, Elmo (1991). *Presidency of Dwight D. Eisenhower*. University Press of Kansas. ISBN 0700604367 OCLC 22307949[89]
- Pickett, William B. (2000). *Eisenhower Decides to Run: Presidential Politics and Cold War Strategy*. Chicago: Ivan R. Dee. ISBN 1-56-663787-2. OCLC 43953970[90].
- Pickett, William B. (1995). *Dwight David Eisenhower and American Power*. Wheeling, Ill.: Harlan Davidson. ISBN 0-88-295918-2. OCLC 31206927[91].
- Watry, David M. (2014). *Diplomacy at the Brink: Eisenhower, Churchill and Eden in the Cold War*. Baton Rouge, LA: Louisiana State University Press.

Historiography and interpretations by scholars

- Burk, Robert. "Eisenhower Revisionism Revisited: Reflections on Eisenhower Scholarship", *Historian*, Spring 1988, Vol. 50, Issue 2, pp. 196–209
- McAuliffe, Mary S. "Eisenhower, the President", *Journal of American History* 68 (1981), pp. 625–32 JSTOR 1901942[92]
- McMahon, Robert J. "Eisenhower and Third World Nationalism: A Critique of the Revisionists," *Political Science Quarterly* (1986) 101#3 pp. 453–73 JSTOR 2151625[93]
- Polsky, Andrew J. "Shifting Currents: Dwight Eisenhower and the Dynamic of Presidential Opportunity Structure," *Presidential Studies Quarterly*, March 2015.
- Rabe, Stephen G. "Eisenhower Revisionism: A Decade of Scholarship," *Diplomatic History* (1993) 17#1 pp 97–115.
- Schlesinger Jr., Arthur. "The Ike Age Revisited," *Reviews in American History* (1983) 11#1 pp. 1–11 JSTOR 2701865[94]
- Streeter, Stephen M. "Interpreting the 1954 U.S. Intervention In Guatemala: Realist, Revisionist, and Postrevisionist Perspectives," *History Teacher* (2000) 34#1 pp 61–74. JSTOR 3054375[95]

Primary sources

- Boyle, Peter G., ed. (1990). *The Churchill–Eisenhower Correspondence, 1953–1955.* University of North Carolina Press.
- Boyle, Peter G., ed. (2005). *The Eden–Eisenhower correspondence, 1955–1957.* University of North Carolina Press. ISBN 0807829358
- Butcher, Harry C. (1946). *My Three Years With Eisenhower The Personal Diary of Captain Harry C. Butcher, USNR*, candid memoir by a top aide
- Eisenhower, Dwight D. (1948). *Crusade in Europe*, his war memoirs.
- Eisenhower, Dwight D. (1963). *Mandate for Change, 1953–1956.*
- Eisenhower, Dwight D. (1965). *The White House Years: Waging Peace 1956–1961*, Doubleday and Co.
- *Eisenhower Papers* 21-volume scholarly edition; complete for 1940–1961.
- Summersby, Kay (1948). *Eisenhower was My Boss*, New York: Prentice Hall; (1949) Dell paperback.

External links

- White House biography[96]
- Eisenhower Presidential Library and Museum[97]
- Eisenhower National Historic Site[98]
- FBI Records: The Vault – Dwight David "Ike" Eisenhower[99]

- Eisenhower Foundation[100]
- Major speeches of Dwight Eisenhower[101]
- "Dwight D. Eisenhower collected news and commentary"[102]. *The New York Times*.
- Dwight D. Eisenhower: A Resource Guide[103] from the Library of Congress
- NATO Declassified – Dwight D. Eisenhower (biography)[104]
- Extensive essays on Dwight Eisenhower[105] and shorter essays on each member of his cabinet and First Lady from the Miller Center of Public Affairs
- "Life Portrait of Dwight D. Eisenhower"[106], from C-SPAN's *American Presidents: Life Portraits*, October 25, 1999
- Works by Dwight David Eisenhower[107] at Project Gutenberg
- Works by Dwight D. Eisenhower[108] at LibriVox (public domain audio-books)
- Works by or about Dwight D. Eisenhower[109] at Internet Archive
- Dwight D. Eisenhower Personal Manuscripts and Letters[110]
- Dwight D. Eisenhower[111] on IMDb
- Appearances[112] on C-SPAN
- Newspaper clippings about Dwight D. Eisenhower[113] in the 20th Century Press Archives of the German National Library of Economics (ZBW)

Presidency

Presidency of Dwight D. Eisenhower

Presidency of Dwight D. Eisenhower	
 Dwight D. Eisenhower, 34th President of the United States	
In office	
January 20, 1953 – January 20, 1961	
Preceded by	Truman presidency
Succeeded by	Kennedy presidency
Seat	White House, Washington, D.C.
Political party	Republican

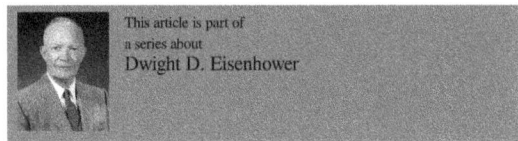

This article is part of a series about
Dwight D. Eisenhower

- Early Life
- Military Career

World War II

Supreme Allied Commander in Europe

- D-Day
- Operation Overlord
- Surrender of Germany
- VE-Day
- *Crusade in Europe*

President of the United States

- Presidency

First Term

- Draft movement
- 1952 Campaign
  - Election
- 1st Inauguration
- Korean War
- Atoms for Peace
- Cold War
  - New Look
  - Domino theory
- Interstate Highway System

Second Term

- 1956 campaign
  - Election
- 2nd Inauguration

- Eisenhower Doctrine
- Sputnik crisis
- Missile gap
- NDEA
- NASA
- DARPA
- Civil Rights Act of 1957
- Little Rock Nine
- U-2 incident
- Farewell Address

Post-Presidency

- Legacy
- Presidential library and museum
- Tributes and memorials

- v
- t
- e[114]

The **presidency of Dwight D. Eisenhower** began on January 20, 1953, when he was inaugurated as the 34th President of the United States, and ended on January 20, 1961. Eisenhower, a Republican, took office as president following a landslide win over Democrat Adlai Stevenson in the 1952 presidential election. This victory upended the New Deal Coalition that had kept the presidency in the hands of the Democratic Party for 20 years. Four years later, in the 1956 presidential election, he defeated Stevenson in a landslide again, winning a second term in office. He was succeeded in office by Democrat John F. Kennedy after the 1960 election.

Eisenhower called for progressive conservativism. That implied that traditional American values included change and progress. Jean Smith says, "He looked to the future, not the past, and his presidency provided a buffered transition from FDR's New Deal and the Fair Deal of Harry Truman into the modern era." Eisenhower was able to secure several victories in Congress, even though Democrats held the majority in both the House and the Senate during all but the first two years of his presidency. Eisenhower continued New Deal programs and expanded Social Security. He took the lead in building the Interstate Highway System in 1956, and the establishment of NASA, with a distinctly civilian (rather than military) mandate. In the Suez Crisis of 1956, Eisenhower used American financial power to force Britain and France to end their occupation of the Suez Canal. Eisenhower signed the first significant civil rights bills of the 20th century, and he sent federal troops to Arkansas to enforce a court ruling mandating school desegregation.

Six months into his first term, the U.S. agreed to an armistice that ended the Korean War. Yet even though at peace, defense spending remained high, as the administration made vigorous efforts to contain the Soviet Union during the Cold War. He authorized covert Central Intelligence Agency actions to overthrow unfriendly governments or protect reliable anti-Communist ones, and he implemented a national security policy that relied on strategic nuclear weapons to deter potential threats, both conventional and nuclear, from Warsaw Pact nations.

Eisenhower was the first U.S. president to be constitutionally limited to two terms under the 22nd Amendment. Voted Gallup's most admired man twelve times, he achieved widespread popular esteem both in and out of office. Since the late 20th century, consensus among Western scholars has consistently held Eisenhower as one of the greatest U.S. Presidents.

Election of 1952

Republican nomination

Dwight D. Eisenhower and Senator Robert A. Taft from Ohio were the two front-runners for the Republican presidential nomination going into the 1952 Republican presidential primaries. Also contending for the nomination were Governor Earl Warren of California, and former Governor Harold Stassen of Minnesota.[115] Taft led the conservative wing of the party, centered in the Midwest, that rejected many of the New Deal social welfare programs created in the 1930s, and generally held a non-interventionist foreign policy stance, believing that America should avoid alliances with foreign powers. Taft had been a candidate for the Republican nomination in 1940 and 1948, but had been defeated both times by moderate Republicans from New York:Wendell Willkie in 1940, and Thomas E. Dewey in 1948. Taft blamed these successive loses on the New York GOP's undue influence over the national party.

Figure 38: *Eisenhower presidential campaign, Baltimore, Maryland, September 1952*

Dewey, the party's presidential nominee in 1944 and 1948, led the moderate wing of the party, centered in the Eastern states. These moderates were generally willing to accept most aspects of the social welfare state created by the New Deal. They also tended to be interventionists in the Cold War, favoring confrontation with the Soviet Union in Eurasia. Dewey, who declined the notion of a third run for president, and other Eastern moderates were determined to use their influence to ensure that the 1952 presidential ticket reflected their views. To this end, a draft Eisenhower organization was assembled, beginning in September 1951. Two weeks later, at the National Governors' Conference meeting, seven Republican governors endorsed his candidacy.[116] Eisenhower, then serving as the Supreme Allied Commander of NATO, had long been mentioned as a possible presidential contender, but he was reluctant to become involved in partisan politics.[117] Foreign policy concerns are what gave impetus to Eisenhower's ultimate entry into the race. He was troubled by Taft's non-interventionist views, especially his opposition to NATO. Eisenhower wholeheartedly supported NATO, which he considered an important deterrence against Soviet aggression.[118] He was also motivated by the corruption that had crept into the federal government during the later years of the Truman administration; believing that the time had come to "clean out the courthouse."[119] Eisenhower indicated in late 1951 that he would not oppose any effort to nominate him for president, although he still refused to openly seek the nomination.[120]

In January 1952, Senator Henry Cabot Lodge Jr. announced that Eisenhower's name would be entered in the March New Hampshire primary, even though he had not yet officially entered the race.[115] The result in New Hampshire was a solid Eisenhower victory with 46,661 votes to 35,838 for Taft and 6,574 for Stassen.[121] In April, Eisenhower resigned from his NATO command and returned to the United States. The Taft forces put up a strong fight in the remaining primaries, and prior to the July 1952 Republican National Convention it was unclear whether Taft or Eisenhower would win the presidential nomination.[122]

When the 1952 Republican National Convention opened in Chicago, Eisenhower's managers accused Taft of "stealing" delegate votes in Southern states such as Texas and Georgia. They claimed that Taft's leaders in these states had unfairly denied delegate spots to Eisenhower supporters and put Taft delegates in their place. Lodge and Dewey proposed to evict the pro-Taft delegates in these states and replace them with pro-Eisenhower delegates; they called this proposal "Fair Play." Although Taft and his supporters angrily denied this charge, the convention voted to support Fair Play 658 to 548, and Taft lost many Southern delegates. Eisenhower also received two more boosts, firstly when several uncommitted state delegations, such as Michigan and Pennsylvania, decided to support him, and secondly when Stassen released his delegates and asked them to support Eisenhower, whose moderate policies he much preferred to those of Taft. The removal of many pro-Taft Southern delegates and the support of the uncommitted states decided the nomination in Eisenhower's favor, which he won on the first ballot. Afterward, Senator Richard Nixon of California was nominated by acclamation as his vice-presidential running mate.[123] Nixon, whose name came to the forefront early and frequently in pre-convention conversations among Eisenhower's campaign managers, was selected because of his relative youth (39 years old) and solid anti-communist credentials.[124]

General election

Incumbent President Harry S. Truman announced his retirement in March 1952, making it unclear who would win the Democratic presidential nomination.[125] Delegates to the 1952 Democratic National Convention, also held in Chicago, nominated Illinois governor Adlai E. Stevenson for president on the third ballot. Senator John Sparkman of Alabama was selected as his running mate. The convention ended with widespread confidence that in Stevenson, the party had selected its ablest candidate, one who would make a powerful presidential contender.[126] Stevenson concentrated on giving a series of thoughtful speeches around the nation. Although his style thrilled intellectuals and academics, some political experts wondered if he were speaking "over the heads" of most of his listeners, and they dubbed him an "egghead," based on his baldness and intellectual demeanor. His biggest liability however, was the unpopularity of the incumbent president, Harry Truman. Even though Stevenson had not had been a part of the Truman administration, voters largely ignored his record and burdened him with Truman's. Historian Herbert Parmet says that Stevenson: <templatestyles src="Template:Quote/styles.css"/>

> *failed to dispel the widespread recognition that, for a divided America, torn by paranoia and unable to understand what had disrupted the anticipated tranquility of the postwar world, the time for change had really arrived. Neither Stevenson nor anyone else could have dissuaded the electorate from its desire to repudiate 'Trumanism.'*

Republican strategy during the fall campaign focused on Eisenhower's unrivaled popularity.[127] Ike traveled to 45 of the 48 states; his heroic image and plain talk excited the large crowds who heard him speak from the campaign train's caboose. In his speeches, Eisenhower never mentioned Stevenson by name, rather, he relentlessly attacked Truman, emphasizing three Truman administration failures: Korea, Communism, and corruption. In addition to the speeches, he got his message out to voters through 30-second television advertisements; this was the first presidential election in which television played a major role. In domestic policy, Eisenhower attacked the growing influence of the federal government in the economy, while in foreign affairs, he supported a strong American role in stemming the expansion of Communism. Eisenhower adopted much of the rhetoric and positions of the contemporary GOP, and many of his public statements were designed to win over conservative supporters of Taft.[128]

A potentially devastating allegation hit when Nixon was accused by several newspapers of receiving $18,000 in undeclared "gifts" from wealthy California donors. In reality, contributions were by design only from early supporters and limited to $1,000, with full accountability. Eisenhower and his aides considered dropping Nixon from the ticket and picking another running mate. Nixon responded to the allegations in a nationally televised speech, the "Checkers speech," on September 23. In this speech, Nixon denied the charges against him, gave a detailed account of his modest financial assets, and offered a glowing assessment of Eisenhower's candidacy. The highlight of the speech came when Nixon stated that a supporter had given his daughters a gift—a dog named "Checkers"—and that he would not return it, because his daughters loved it. The public responded to the speech with an outpouring of support, and Eisenhower stayed with him.[129]

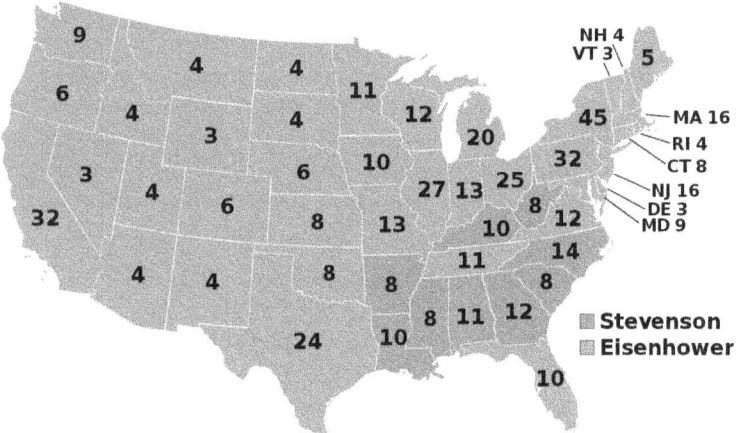

Figure 39: *1952 electoral vote results*

In the end, the burden of the ongoing Korean War, Communist threat, and Truman scandals, was too much for Stevenson to overcome. On election day, Eisenhower won a landslide victory, winning 55.2 percent of the popular vote and 442 electoral votes. Stevenson received 44.5 percent of the popular vote and 89 electoral votes.[130] Eisenhower won every state outside of the South, as well as Virginia, Florida, and Texas, each of which voted Republican for just the second time since the end of Reconstruction. In the concurrent congressional elections, Republicans won control of the House of Representatives and the Senate.[131]

Administration

Cabinet

The Eisenhower Cabinet		
Office	Name	Term
President	Dwight D. Eisenhower	1953–1961
Vice President	Richard Nixon	1953–1961
Secretary of State	John Foster Dulles	1953–1959
	Christian A. Herter	1959–1961

Secretary of Treasury	George M. Humphrey	1953–1957
	Robert B. Anderson	1957–1961
Secretary of Defense	Charles E. Wilson	1953–1957
	Neil H. McElroy	1957–1959
	Thomas S. Gates Jr.	1959–1961
Attorney General	Herbert Brownell	1953–1957
	William P. Rogers	1957–1961
Postmaster General	Arthur E. Summerfield	1953–1961
Secretary of the Interior	Douglas McKay	1953–1956
	Fred A. Seaton	1956–1961
Secretary of Agriculture	Ezra Taft Benson	1953–1961
Secretary of Commerce	Sinclair Weeks	1953–1958
	Lewis L. Strauss	1958–1959
	Frederick H. Mueller	1959–1961
Secretary of Labor	Martin P. Durkin	1953
	James P. Mitchell	1953–1961
Secretary of Health, Education, and Welfare	Oveta Culp Hobby	1953–1955
	Marion B. Folsom	1955–1958
	Arthur S. Flemming	1958–1961

Regarding Eisenhower's administrative style as president, historian Samuel Eliot Morison wrote, <templatestyles src="Template:Quote/styles.css"/>

The President organized his administration somewhat like a military staff. Men below him were supposed to work out in detail what needed to be done; the President had to make the ultimate decision, but he disliked doing any preliminary thinking about it himself. Contradictory recommendations would come to him on defense and other matters from two or three different departments, each already watered down while passing up from lower echelons. The President, who studied no problem deeply himself, would return the differing recommendations and offer an all-round agreement on which to base his decision; thus almost every decision was a compromise, and often a wishy-washy compromise.[132]

Eisenhower delegated the selection of his cabinet to two close associates, Lucius D. Clay and Herbert Brownell Jr.; Brownell, a legal aid to Dewey, became attorney general. John Foster Dulles, an attorney who also had close ties to Dewey, became the secretary of state.[133] A conscientious "student of foreign affairs," Dulles had previously had a part in developing the both the United Nations Charter and the Treaty of San Francisco. He traveled nearly 560,000 miles (901,233 km) during his six years in office.[132] Outside of the cabinet, Eisenhower selected Sherman Adams as White House Chief of Staff, while Milton S. Eisenhower, the president's brother and a prominent college administrator, emerged as an important adviser.[134] Eisenhower also elevated the role of the National Security Council, and Robert Cutler served as the first National Security Advisor.[135]

Eisenhower sought out leaders of big business for many of his other cabinet appointments. Charles Erwin Wilson, the CEO of General Motors, was Eisenhower's first secretary of defense. In 1957, he was replaced by president of Procter & Gamble president, Neil H. McElroy. For the position of secretary of the treasury, Ike selected George M. Humphrey, the CEO of several steel and coal companies. His postmaster general, Arthur E. Summerfield, and first secretary of the interior, Douglas McKay, were both automobile distributors. Additionally, former senator, Sinclair Weeks, director of the National Association of Manufacturers.[132,133] Eisenhower appointed Joseph Dodge, a longtime bank president who also had extensive government experience, as the director of the Bureau of the Budget, and Dodge was the first budget director to be given cabinet-level status.[136] Several businessmen named to cabinet-level posts—Wilson, Humphrey, along with Harold E. Talbott (Eisenhower's first Air Force secretary) and Robert Tripp Ross, (a deputy assistant secretary of defense)—came under U.S. Senate scrutiny due their investments and possible conflicts of interest while in office; Talbott and Ross later resigned as a result.[132]

Other Eisenhower cabinet selections were made to cover various "political bases." Ezra Taft Benson, a high-ranking member of The Church of Jesus Christ of Latter-day Saints, was chosen as secretary of agriculture; he was the only person appointed from the Taft wing of the party. Oveta Culp Hobby became the first secretary of the newly created Department of Health, Education, and Welfare; she was the second female cabinet secretary (after Frances Perkins). Martin Patrick Durkin, a Democrat and president of the plumbers and steamfitters union, was selected as secretary of labor.[132,133] As a result, it became a standing joke that his first Cabinet was composed of "nine millionaires and a plumber." Dissatisfied with Eisenhower's labor policies, Durkin resigned after less than a year in office, and was replaced by James P. Mitchell.[137]

Vice-presidency

Eisenhower, who disliked partisan politics and politicians,[132] left much of the building and sustaining of the Republican Party to his Vice President Nixon. Additionally, shocked at how ill-prepared Vice President Truman had been on major issues such as the atomic bomb when he acceded to the presidency, Eisenhower therefore made sure to keep Nixon fully involved. He gave Nixon multiple diplomatic, domestic, and political assignments so that he "evolved into one of Ike's most valuable subordinates." The office of vice president was thereby fundamentally upgraded from a minor ceremonial post to a major role in the presidential team. Nixon went well beyond the assignment. "Nixon threw himself into state and local politics, making hundreds of speeches across the land. With Eisenhower uninvolved in party building, Nixon became the *de facto* national GOP leader."

Press corps

Eisenhower frequently met with the press corps, but his performance in these meetings was widely regarded as awkward. These press conferences contributed greatly to the criticism that Eisenhower was ill-informed or merely a figurehead in his government. At times, he was able to use his reputation for unintelligible press conferences to his advantage, as it allowed him to obfuscate his position on difficult subjects.[138] On January 19, 1955 Eisenhower became the first president to conduct a televised news conference. His press secretary, James Campbell Hagerty, is the only person to have served in that capacity for two full presidential terms. Historian Robert Hugh Ferrell considered him to be the best press secretary in presidential history, because he "organized the presidency for the single innovation in press relations that has itself almost changed the nature of the nation's highest office in recent decades."

Continuity of government

A group of three federal government officials and six private U.S. citizens was secretly tasked by the president in 1958 to serve as federal administrators in the event of a national emergency, such as a nuclear attack. Eisenhower discussed the issues with each appointee and then personally sent letters of confirmation. The selection and appointment of these administrator-designates was classified Top Secret. In an emergency, each administrator was to take charge of a specifically activated agency to maintain the continuity of government. Named to the group were:

Figure 40: *Earl Warren, the 14th Chief Justice of the United States, presided over the liberal Warren Court from October 1953 until June 1969.*[139]

- Theodore F. Koop, Vice President of CBS – Emergency Censorship Agency
- Frank Stanton, President of CBS – Emergency Communications Agency
- John Ed Warren, Senior Vice President of First National City Bank – Emergency Energy and Minerals Agency
- Ezra Taft Benson, Secretary of Agriculture – Emergency Food Agency
- Aksel Nielsen, President of Title Guaranty Company – Emergency Housing Agency
- James P. Mitchell, Secretary of Labor – Emergency Manpower Agency
- Harold Boeschenstein, President of Owens-Corning Fiberglass – Emergency Production Agency
- William McChesney Martin, Chairman of the Federal Reserve Board of Governors – Emergency Stabilization Agency
- Frank Pace, Executive Vice President of General Dynamics – Emergency Transport Agency (resigned January 8, 1959)
- George P. Baker, Dean of Harvard Business School – Emergency Transport Agency (after January 8, 1959)

Judicial appointments

Eisenhower appointed five Justices of the Supreme Court of the United States. In 1953, Eisenhower nominated Governor Earl Warren to succeed Chief Justice Fred M. Vinson. Many conservative Republicans opposed Warren's nomination, but they were unable to block the appointment, and Warren's nomination was approved by the Senate in January 1954. Warren presided over a court that generated numerous liberal rulings on various topics, beginning in 1954 with the desegregation case of *Brown v. Board of Education*.[140] Robert H. Jackson's death in late 1954 generated another vacancy on the Supreme Court, and Eisenhower successfully nominated federal appellate judge John Marshall Harlan II to succeed Jackson. Harlan joined the conservative bloc on the bench, often supporting the position of Associate Justice Felix Frankfurter.

After Sherman Minton resigned in 1956, Eisenhower nominated state supreme court justice William J. Brennan to the Supreme Court. Eisenhower hoped that the appointment of Brennan, a liberal-leaning Catholic, would boost his own re-election campaign. Opposition from Senator Joseph McCarthy and others delayed Brennan's confirmation, so Eisenhower placed Brennan on the court via a recess appointment in 1956; the Senate confirmed Brennan's nomination in early 1957. Brennan joined Warren as a leader of the court's liberal bloc. Stanley Reed's retirement in 1957 created another vacancy, and Eisenhower nominated federal appellate judge Charles Evans Whittaker, who would serve on the Supreme Court for just five years before resigning. The fifth and final Supreme Court vacancy of Eisenhower's tenure arose in 1958 due to the retirement of Harold Burton. Eisenhower successfully nominated federal appellate judge Potter Stewart to succeed Burton, and Stewart became a centrist on the court. Eisenhower also appointed 45 judges to the United States Courts of Appeals, and 129 judges to the United States district courts.

Foreign affairs

Cold War

For three decades Eisenhower had designed increasingly complex war plans. Upon taking office as president, he now set himself to designing the basic American strategy for fighting the Cold War against world communism. Eisenhower planned for the full mobilization of American society, and especially the technological superiority to promote military preparedness, intelligence services, and covert action by the CIA. According to biographer William I. Hitchcock, he planned:

> Elaborate security measures to combat domestic spying....a nationwide manpower program, emphasizing scientific and technical training to serve

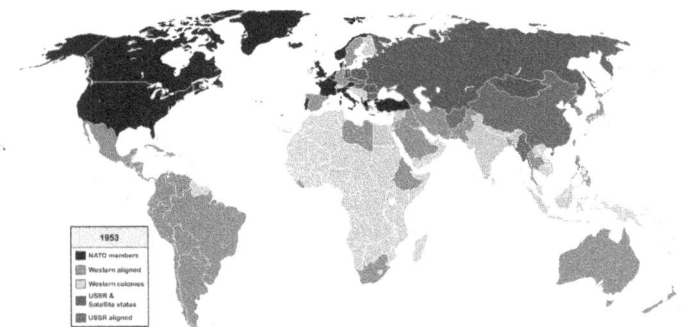

Figure 41: *A map of the geopolitical situation in 1953*

military needs....stockpiling and securing of vital raw materials and key industrial plants....huge continental defense systems, with early warning radar and a large air force that could meet Soviet intruders.... Longer tours of duty for draftees, inclusion of women into the armed services....[and] a better public effort to explain to the American people why such a militaristic mobilization of their society was needed.[141]

The Cold War dominated international politics in the 1950s. As both the United States and the Soviet Union possessed nuclear weapons, any conflict presented the risk of escalation into nuclear warfare.[142] Eisenhower continued the basic Truman administration policy of containment of Soviet expansion and the strengthening of the economies of Western Europe. Eisenhower's overall Cold War policy was described by NSC 174, which held that the rollback of Soviet influence was a long-term goal, but that the United States would not provoke war with the Soviet Union.[143]

Joseph Stalin died in March 1953, and Georgy Malenkov took leadership of the Soviet Union. Malenkov proposed a "peaceful coexistence" with the West, and British Prime Minister Winston Churchill proposed a summit of the world leaders. Fearing that the summit would delay the rearmament of West Germany, and skeptical of Malenkov's intentions and ability to stay in power, the Eisenhower administration nixed the summit idea. In April, Eisenhower delivered his "Chance for Peace speech," in which he called for an armistice in Korea, free elections to re-unify Germany, the "full independence" of Eastern European nations, and United Nations control of atomic energy. Though well received in the West as the marking the beginning of dialogue between the Western bloc and the Eastern bloc, the Soviet leadership viewed Eisenhower's speech as little more than propaganda. In 1954, a more confrontational leader took charge in the Soviet Union, Nikita Khrushchev. Eisenhower became increasingly skeptical of the possibility of cooperation with the Soviet Union

Figure 42: *Eisenhower and members of his Cabinet inspect the YB-52 prototype of the B-52, c.1954*

after it refused to support his Atoms for Peace proposal, which called for the creation of the International Atomic Energy Agency and the creation of nuclear power plants.[144]

New Look policy

The administration's initial national security policy, referred to as New Look, was unveiled on October 30, 1953. The product of a series of meetings with senior cabinet-level officials, consultations with National Security Council personnel (Project Solarium), and a comprehensive defense review by the Joint Chiefs of Staff, it reflected Eisenhower's desire for a sustainable long-term U.S. national security policy, and also his belief that the mission of the military was to "get ready and stay ready." The National Security Council document upon which the policy was built, NSC 162/2, emphasized reliance on strategic nuclear weapons to deter potential threats, both conventional and nuclear, from the Soviet Union and its Eastern Bloc allies. The document also called for reductions in defense spending and foreign aid, basing these recommendations on the argument that a healthy economy "relies at the very basis of a sound capability for defense."[145] Nuclear weapons were seen as the most economically feasible means to deter the Soviet advantage in Europe infantry and tanks. The U.S. military developed a strategy of nuclear deterrence based upon the triad of land-based intercontinental ballistic missiles (ICBMs), strategic bombers, and submarine-launched ballistic missiles (SLBMs). Throughout his presidency, Eisenhower insisted on having plans to retaliate, fight, and win a nuclear war against the Soviets, although he hoped he would never feel forced to use such weapons.

As the ground war in Korea ended, Eisenhower sharply reduced the reliance on expensive Army divisions. Historian Saki Dockrill argues that his long-term strategy was to promote the collective security of NATO and other American allies, strengthen the Third World against Soviet pressures, avoid another Korea, and produce a climate that would slowly and steadily weaken Soviet power and influence. Dockrill points to Eisenhower's use of multiple assets against the Soviet Union: <templatestyles src="Template:Quote/styles.css"/>

Eisenhower knew that the United States had many other assets that could be translated into influence over the Soviet bloc—its democratic values and institutions, its rich and competitive capitalist economy, its intelligence technology and skills in obtaining information as to the enemy's capabilities and intentions, its psychological warfare and covert operations capabilities, its negotiating skills, and its economic and military assistance to the Third World.

End of the Korean War

During his campaign, Eisenhower said he would go to Korea to end the Korean War, which had broken out in 1950 after North Korea invaded South Korea.[146] The U.S. had joined the war to prevent the fall of South Korea, but the intervention of Chinese forces in late 1950 led to a protracted stalemate.[147] Truman had begun in peace talks in mid-1951, but the issue of North Korean and Chinese prisoners remained a sticking point. Over 40,000 prisoners from the two countries refused repatriation, but North Korea and China nonetheless demanded their return.[148] Upon taking office, Eisenhower demanded a solution, and decided to warn China that he would use nuclear weapons to resolve the problem. China came to terms, and an armistice was signed on July 27, 1953 as the Korean Armistice Agreement. Historian Edward C. Keefer says that in accepting the American demands that POWs could refuse to return to their home country, "China and North Korea still swallowed the bitter pill, probably forced down in part by the atomic ultimatum."[149] The armistice led to decades of uneasy peace between North Korea and South Korea. The United States and South Korea signed a defensive treaty in October 1953, and the U.S. continued to station thousands of soldiers in South Korea after the end of the Korean War.[150]

Covert actions

Eisenhower, while accepting the doctrine of containment, sought to counter the Soviet Union through more active means as detailed in the State-Defense report NSC 68. The Eisenhower administration developed the tactic of covert action, used by the Central Intelligence Agency to interfere with suspected communist governments abroad. An early use of covert action was against the elected Prime Minister of Iran, Mohammed Mosaddeq. The Shah of Iran and pro-monarchy forces ejected him from power in the complex 1953 Iranian coup d'état (Operation Ajax). The CIA also instigated the 1954 Guatemalan coup d'état by the local military that overthrew president Jacobo Arbenz Guzmán. The U.S. complaint was that he was veering toward the Soviet Union. Critics have produced conspiracy theories about the causal factors, but according to historian Stephen M. Streeter, CIA documents show the United Fruit Company (UFCO) played no major role in Eisenhower's decision, that Soviet influence was also minimal, and that the Eisenhower administration did not need to be forced into the action by any lobby groups. Streeter Identifies three major interpretive perspectives, "Realist," "Revisionist," and "Postrevisionist':

> Realists, who concern themselves primarily with power politics, have generally blamed the Cold War on an aggressive, expansionist Soviet empire. Because realists believe that Arbenz was a Soviet puppet, they view his overthrow as the necessary rollback of communism in the Western Hemisphere. Revisionists, who place the majority of the blame for the Cold War on the United States, emphasize how Washington sought to expand overseas markets and promote foreign investment, especially in the Third World. Revisionists allege that because the State Department came to the rescue of the UFCO, the U.S. intervention in Guatemala represents a prime example of economic imperialism. Postrevisionists, a difficult group to define precisely, incorporate both strategic and economic factors in their interpretation of the Cold War. They tend to agree with revisionists on the issue of Soviet responsibility, but they are much more concerned with explaining the cultural and ideological influences that warped Washington's perception of the Communist threat. According to postrevisionists, the Eisenhower administration officials turned against Arbenz because they failed to grasp that he represented a nationalist rather than a communist.[151]

Proposed Bricker Amendment

In January 1953, Senator John W. Bricker of Ohio re-introduced the Bricker Amendment, which would limit the president's treaty making power and ability to enter into executive agreements with foreign nations. Fears that the steady stream of post-World War II-era international treaties, pacts, covenants, and executive agreements entered into by the U.S. government were supplanting the U.S. Constitution as the supreme law of the land, and undermining the nation's sovereignty, united isolationists, conservative Democrats, most Republicans, along with numerous professional groups and civic organizations behind the amendment. Eisenhower opposed the amendment, believing that it would weaken the president and would hamper the handling of the nation's foreign affairs to such a degree, that it would be impossible for the U.S. to exercise leadership on the global stage. Eisenhower worked with Senate Minority Lyndon B. Johnson to defeat the amendment.[152] Although the amendment started out with 56 co-sponsors, it went down to defeat in the U.S. Senate in 1954, with a 42-50 vote. Later in 1954, a watered-down version of the amendment missed the required two-thirds majority in the Senate by one vote. This episode proved to be the last hurrah for the isolationist Republicans, as younger conservatives increasingly turned to an internationalism based on aggressive anti-communism, typified by Senator Barry Goldwater.

Europe

Eisenhower sought troop reductions in Europe by sharing of defense responsibilities with NATO allies. Europeans, however, never quite trusted the idea of nuclear deterrence and were reluctant to shift away from NATO into a proposed European Defence Community (EDC). Like Truman, Eisenhower believed that the rearmament of West Germany was vital to NATO's strategic interests. The administration backed an arrangement devised by Churchill and British Foreign Minister Anthony Eden in which West Germany was rearmed, became a fully sovereign member of NATO, and promised not to establish atomic, biological, or chemical weapons programs. European leaders also created the Western European Union to coordinate European defense. In response to the integration of West Germany into NATO, Eastern bloc leaders established the Warsaw Pact. Austria, which had been jointly-occupied by the Soviet Union and the Western powers, regained its sovereignty with the 1955 Austrian State Treaty. As part of the arrangement that ended the occupation, Austria declared its neutrality after gaining independence.[153]

The Eisenhower administration placed a high priority on undermining Soviet influence on Eastern Europe, and escalated a propaganda war under the leadership of Charles Douglas Jackson. The United States dropped over 300,000 propaganda leaflets in Eastern Europe between 1951 and 1956, and Radio Free Europe sent broadcasts throughout the region. A 1953 uprising in East Germany briefly stoked the administration's hopes of a decline in Soviet influence, but the USSR quickly crushed the insurrection. In 1956, a major uprising broke out in Hungary. After Hungarian leader Imre Nagy promised the institution of multiparty democracy and a withdrawal from the Warsaw Pact,

Figure 43: *With Republic of China President Chiang Kai-shek, Eisenhower waved to Taiwanese people during his visit to Taipei, Taiwan in June 1960.*

Soviet leader Nikita Khrushchev dispatched 60,000 soldiers into Hungary, and the rebellion was violently crushed. The United States strongly condemned the military response but did not take direct action, disappointing many Hungarian revolutionaries. After the revolution, the United States shifted from encouraging revolt to seeking cultural and economic ties as a means of undermining Communist regimes.[154]

In 1953, Eisenhower opened relations with Spain under dictator Francisco Franco. Despite its undemocratic nature, Spain's strategic position in light of the Cold War and anti-communist position led Eisenhower to build a trade and military alliance with the Spanish through the Pact of Madrid. These relations brought an end to Spain's isolation after World War II, which in turn led to a Spanish economic boom known as the Spanish miracle.

East Asia and Southeast Asia

After the end of World War II, the Communist Việt Minh launched an insurrection against French-supported State of Vietnam.[155] Seeking to bolster France and prevent the fall of Vietnam to Communism, the Truman and Eisenhower administrations played a major role in financing French military operations in Vietnam.[156] In 1954, the French requested the United States to intervene in the Battle of Dien Bien Phu, which would prove to be the climactic battle of the First Indochina War. Seeking to rally public support for the intervention, Eisenhower articulated the domino theory, which held that the fall of Vietnam could lead to the fall of other countries. As France refused to commit to an independent Vietnam, Congress refused to approve of the intervention, and the French were defeated at Dien Bien Phu. In the contemporaneous Geneva Conference, Dulles convinced Chinese and Soviet leaders to pressure Viet Minh leaders to accept the temporary partition of Vietnam. Vietnam was divided into a Communist northern half (under Ho Chi Minh) and a non-Communist southern half (under Ngo Dinh Diem).[155] Despite some doubts about the strength of Diem's government, the Eisenhower administration directed aid to South Vietnam in hopes of creating a bulwark against further Communist expansion.[157] With Eisenhower's approval, Diem refused to hold elections to re-unify Vietnam; those elections had been scheduled for 1956 as part of the agreement at the Geneva Conference.[158]

Eisenhower's commitment in South Vietnam was part of a broader program to contain China and the Soviet Union in East Asia. In 1954, the United States and seven other countries created the Southeast Asia Treaty Organization (SEATO), a defensive alliance dedicated to preventing the spread of Communism in Southeast Asia. In 1954, China began shelling tiny islands off the coast of Mainland China which were controlled by the Republic of China (ROC). The shelling nearly escalated to nuclear war as Eisenhower considered using nuclear weapons to prevent the invasion of Taiwan, the main island controlled by the ROC. The crisis ended when China ended the shelling and both sides agreed to diplomatic talks; a second crisis in 1958 would end in a similar fashion. During the first crisis, the United States and the ROC signed the Sino-American Mutual Defense Treaty, which committed the United States to the defense of Taiwan.[159] The CIA also supported dissidents in the 1959 Tibetan uprising, but China crushed the uprising.[160]

Middle East

The Middle East became increasingly important to U.S. foreign policy during the 1950s. After the 1953 Iranian coup, the U.S. supplanted Britain as the most influential ally of Iran. Eisenhower encouraged the creation of the Baghdad Pact, a military alliance consisting of Turkey, Iran, Iraq, and Pakistan. As it did in several other regions, the Eisenhower administration sought to establish stable, friendly, anti-Communist regimes in the Arab World. The U.S. attempted to mediate the Israeli–Palestinian conflict, but Israel's unwillingness to give up its gains from the 1948 Arab–Israeli War and Arab hostility towards Israel scuttled the possibility of an agreement.[161]

Suez crisis

In 1952, a revolution led by Gamal Abdel Nasser had overthrown the pro-British Egyptian government. After taking power as Prime Minister of Egypt in 1954, Nasser played the Soviet Union and the United States against each other, seeking aid from both sides. Eisenhower sought to bring Nasser into the American sphere of influence through economic aid, but Nasser's Arab nationalism and opposition to Israel served as a source of friction between the United States and Egypt. One of Nasser's main goals was the construction of the Aswan Dam, which would provide immense hydroelectric power and help irrigate much of Egypt. Eisenhower attempted to use American aid for the financing of the construction of the dam as leverage for other areas of foreign policy, but aid negotiations collapsed. In July 1956, just a week after the collapse of the aid negotiations, Nasser nationalized the British-run Suez Canal, sparking the Suez Crisis.[162]

The British strongly protested the nationalization, and formed a plan with France and Israel to capture the canal.[163] Eisenhower opposed military intervention, and he repeatedly told British Prime Minister Anthony Eden that the U.S. would not tolerate an invasion.[164] Though opposed to the nationalization of the canal, Eisenhower feared that a military intervention would disrupt global trade and alienate Middle Eastern countries from the West.[165] Israel attacked Egypt in October 1956, quickly seizing control of the Sinai Peninsula. France and Britain launched air and naval attacks after Nasser refused to renounce Egypt's nationalization of the canal. Nasser responded by sinking dozens of ships, preventing operation of the canal. Angered by the attacks, which risked sending Arab states into the arms of the Soviet Union, the Eisenhower administration proposed a cease fire and used economic pressure to force France and Britain to withdraw.[166] The incident marked the end of British and French dominance in the Middle East and opened the way for greater American involvement in the region. In early 1958, Eisenhower used the threat of economic sanctions to coerce Israel into withdrawing from the Sinai Peninsula, and the Suez Canal resumed operations under the control of Egypt.[167]

Eisenhower Doctrine

In response to the power vacuum in the Middle East following the Suez Crisis, the Eisenhower administration developed a new policy to guide U.S. intervention to stabilize the region against Soviet threats or internal turmoil or revolution. Given the collapse of British prestige and the rise of Soviet interest in the region, the president informed Congress on January 5, 1957 that it was essential for the U.S. to accept new responsibilities for the security of the Middle East. Under the policy, known as the Eisenhower Doctrine, any Middle

Eastern country could request American economic assistance or aid from U.S. military forces if it was being threatened by armed aggression. Eisenhower found it difficult to convince leading Arab states or Israel to endorse the doctrine's purpose or usefulness. Nonetheless, he applied the doctrine in 1957-58 by dispensing economic aid to shore up the Kingdom of Jordan, by encouraging Syria's neighbors to consider military operations against it, and by sending U.S. troops into Lebanon to prevent a radical revolution from sweeping over that country. Though the troops sent to Lebanon never saw any fighting, the deployment marked the only time during Eisenhower's presidency when U.S. troops were sent abroad into a potential combat situation.[168]

Though U.S. aid helped Lebanon and Jordan avoid revolution, the Eisenhower doctrine enhanced Nasser's prestige as the preeminent Arab nationalist. Partly as a result of the bungled U.S. intervention in Syria, Nasser established the short-lived United Arab Republic, a political union between Egypt and Syria.[169] The U.S. also lost a sympathetic Middle Eastern government due to the 1958 Iraqi coup d'état, which saw King Faisal I replaced by General Abd al-Karim Qasim as the leader of Iraq.[170]

South Asia

The 1947 partition of British India created two new independent states, India and Pakistan. Indian Prime Minister Jawaharlal Nehru pursued a non-aligned policy in the Cold War, and frequently criticized U.S. policies. Largely out of a desire to build up military strength against the more populous India, Pakistan sought close relations with the United States. Pakistan became a U.S. ally in the Cold War, joining both the Baghdad Pact and SEATO. This U.S.-Pakistan alliance alienated India from the United States, and India moved closer to the Soviet Union. In the late 1950s, the Eisenhower administration sought closer relations with India, sending aid to stem the 1957 Indian economic crisis. By the end of his administration, relations between the United States and India had moderately improved, but Pakistan remained the main U.S. ally in South Asia.[171]

Latin America

For much of his administration, Eisenhower largely continued the policy of his predecessors in Latin America, supporting U.S.-friendly governments regardless of whether they held power through authoritarian means. The Eisenhower administration expanded military aid to Latin America, and used Pan-Americanism as a tool to prevent the spread of Soviet influence. In the late 1950s, several Latin American governments fell, partly due to a recession in the United States.[172]

Figure 44: *First test launch of the PGM-17 Thor from Cape Canaveral Launch Complex 17B, January 25, 1957*

Cuba was particularly close to the United States, and 300,000 American tourists visited Cuba each year in the late 1950s. Cuban President Fulgencio Batista sought close ties with both the U.S. government and major U.S. companies, and American organized crime also had a strong presence in Cuba.[173] In January 1959, the Cuban Revolution ousted Batista. The new regime, led by Fidel Castro, quickly legalized the Communist Party of Cuba, sparking U.S. fears that Castro would align with the Soviet Union. When Castro visited the United States in April 1959, Eisenhower refused to meet with him, delegating the task to Nixon.[174] In the aftermath of the Cuban Revolution, the Eisenhower administration began to encourage democratic government in Latin America and increased economic aid to the region. As Castro drew closer to the Soviet Union, the U.S. broke diplomatic relations, launched a near-total embargo, and began preparations for an invasion of Cuba by Cuban exiles.[175]

Ballistic missiles and arms control

As part of his administration's New Look policy, Eisenhower presided over the development of ballistic missiles and nuclear warheads. The number of nuclear weapons possessed by the United States grew from 1,500 in early 1953 to 6,000 in early 1959.[176] In January 1956 the United States Air Force began developing the Thor, a 1,500 miles (2,400 km) Intermediate-range ballistic missile. The program proceeded quickly, and beginning in 1958 the first of 20 Royal Air Force Thor squadrons became operational in the United Kingdom. This was the first experiment at sharing strategic nuclear weapons in NATO and led to other placements abroad of American nuclear weapons. Critics at the time, led by Democratic Senator John F. Kennedy levied charges to the effect that there was a "missile gap", that is, the U.S. had fallen militarily behind the Soviets because of their lead in space. Historians now discount those allegations, although they agree that Eisenhower did not effectively respond to his critics.[177] In fact, the Soviet Union did not deploy ICBMs until after Eisenhower left office, and the U.S. retained an overall advantage in nuclear weaponry. Eisenhower was aware of the American advantage in ICBM development because of intelligence gathered by U-2 planes, which had begun flying over the Soviet Union in 1956.[178]

The administration decided the best way to minimize the proliferation of nuclear weapons was to tightly control knowledge of gas-centrifuge technology, which was essential to turn ordinary uranium and to weapons-grade uranium. American diplomats by 1960 reached agreement with the German, Dutch, and British governments to limit access to the technology. The four-power understanding on gas-centrifuge secrecy would last until 1975, when scientist Abdul Qadeer Khan took the Dutch centrifuge technology to Pakistan. France sought American help in developing its own nuclear program, but Eisenhower rejected these overtures due to France's instability and his distrust of French leader Charles de Gaulle.[179]

U-2 Crisis

U.S. and Soviet leaders met at the 1955 Geneva Summit, the first such summit since the 1945 Potsdam Conference. No progress was made on major issues; the two sides had major differences on German policy, and the Soviets dismissed Eisenhower's "Open Skies" proposal.[180] Despite the lack of agreement on substantive issues, the conference marked the start of a minor thaw in Cold War relations.[181] Kruschev toured the United States in 1959, and he and Eisenhower conducted high-level talks regarding nuclear disarmament and the status of Berlin. Eisenhower wanted limits on nuclear weapons testing and on-site inspections of nuclear weapons, while Kruschev initially sought the total elimination of nuclear arsenals. Both wanted to limit total military spending and prevent nuclear proliferation, but Cold War tensions made negotiations difficult.[182] Towards the end of his second term, Eisenhower was determined to reach a nuclear test ban treaty as part of an overall move towards détente with the Soviet Union. Khruschev had also become increasingly interested in reaching an accord, partly due to the growing Sino-Soviet split.[183] By 1960,

Figure 45: *Countries visited by Eisenhower during his presidency.*

the major unresolved issue was on-site inspections, as both sides sought nuclear test bans. Hopes for reaching a nuclear agreement agreement at a May 1960 summit in Paris were derailed by the downing of an American U-2 spy plane over the Soviet Union.[182]

The Eisenhower administration, initially thinking the pilot had died in the crash, authorized the release of a cover story claiming that the plane was a "weather research aircraft" which had unintentionally strayed into Soviet airspace after the pilot had radioed "difficulties with his oxygen equipment" while flying over Turkey. Further, Eisenhower said that his administration had not been spying on the Soviet Union; when the Soviets produced the pilot, Captain Francis Gary Powers, the Americans were caught misleading the public, and the incident resulted in international embarrassment for the United States. The Senate Foreign Relations Committee held a lengthy inquiry into the U-2 incident.[184] During the Paris Summit, Eisenhower accused Khrushchev "of sabotaging this meeting, on which so much of the hopes of the world have rested". Later, Eisenhower stated it had all been ruined because of that "stupid U-2 business".

International trips

Eisenhower made one international trip while president-elect, to South Korea, December 2–5, 1952, where he visited Seoul and the Korean combat zone. He also made 16 international trips to 26 nations during his presidency. Between August 1959 and June 1960, he undertook five major tours, travelling to Europe, Southeast Asia, South America, the Middle East, and Southern Asia. On his "Flight to Peace" Goodwill tour, in December 1959, the President visited 11 nations including five in Asia, flying 22,000 miles in 19 days.

	Dates	Country	Locations	Details
1	December 2–5, 1952	South Korea	Seoul	Visit to Korean combat zone. (Visit made as President-elect.)
2	October 19, 1953	Mexico	Nueva Ciudad Guerrero	Dedication of Falcon Dam, with President Adolfo Ruiz Cortines.[185]
3	November 13–15, 1953	Canada	Ottawa	State visit. Met with Governor General Vincent Massey and Prime Minister Louis St. Laurent. Addressed Parliament.
4	December 4–8, 1953	Bermuda	Hamilton	Attended the Bermuda Conference with Prime Minister Winston Churchill and French Prime Minister Joseph Laniel.
5	July 16–23, 1955	Switzerland	Geneva	Attended the Geneva Summit with British Prime Minister Anthony Eden, French Premier Edgar Faure and Soviet Premier Nikolai Bulganin.
6	July 21–23, 1956	Panama	Panama City	Attended the meeting of the presidents of the American republics.
7	March 20–24, 1957	Bermuda	Hamilton	Met with Prime Minister Harold Macmillan.
8	December 14–19, 1957	France	Paris	Attended the First NATO summit.
9	July 8–11, 1958	Canada	Ottawa	Informal visit. Met with Governor General Vincent Massey and Prime Minister John Diefenbaker. Addressed Parliament.
10	February 19–20, 1959	Mexico	Acapulco	Informal meeting with President Adolfo López Mateos.
11	June 26, 1959	Canada	Montreal	Joined Queen Elizabeth II in ceremony opening the St. Lawrence Seaway.
12	August 26–27, 1959	West Germany	Bonn	Informal meeting with Chancellor Konrad Adenauer and President Theodor Heuss.
	August 27 – September 2, 1959	United Kingdom	London, Balmoral, Chequers	Informal visit. Met Prime Minister Harold Macmillan and Queen Elizabeth II.
	September 2–4, 1959	France	Paris	Informal meeting with President Charles de Gaulle and Italian Prime Minister Antonio Segni. Addressed North Atlantic Council.
	September 4–7, 1959	United Kingdom	Culzean Castle	Rested before returning to the United States.
13	December 4–6, 1959	Italy	Rome	Informal visit. Met with President Giovanni Gronchi.

	Date	Country	City	Details
	December 6, 1959	Vatican City	Apostolic Palace	Audience with Pope John XXIII.
	December 6–7, 1959	Turkey	Ankara	Informal visit. Met with President Celâl Bayar.
	December 7–9, 1959	Pakistan	Karachi	Informal visit. Met with President Ayub Khan.
	December 9, 1959	Afghanistan	Kabul	Informal visit. Met with King Mohammed Zahir Shah.
	December 9–14, 1959	India	New Delhi, Agra	Met with President Rajendra Prasad and Prime Minister Jawaharlal Nehru. Addressed Parliament.
	December 14, 1959	Iran	Tehran	Met with Shah Mohammad Reza Pahlavi. Addressed Parliament.
	December 14–15, 1959	Greece	Athens	Official visit. Met with King Paul and Prime Minister Konstantinos Karamanlis. Addressed Parliament.
	December 17, 1959	Tunisia	Tunis	Met with President Habib Bourguiba.
	December 18–21, 1959	France	Toulon, Paris	Conference with President Charles de Gaulle, British Prime Minister Harold Macmillan and German Chancellor Konrad Adenauer.
	December 21–22, 1959	Spain	Madrid	Met with Generalissimo Francisco Franco.
	December 22, 1959	Morocco	Casablanca	Met with King Mohammed V.
14	February 23–26, 1960	Brazil	Brasília, Rio de Janeiro, São Paulo	Met with President Juscelino Kubitschek. Addressed Brazilian Congress.
	February 26–29, 1960	Argentina	Buenos Aires, Mar del Plata, San Carlos de Bariloche	Met with President Arturo Frondizi.
	February 29 – March 2, 1960	Chile	Santiago	Met with President Jorge Alessandri.
	March 2–3, 1960	Uruguay	Montevideo	Met with President Benito Nardone. Returned to the U.S. via Buenos Aires and Suriname.
15	May 15–19, 1960	France	Paris	Conference with President Charles de Gaulle, British Prime Minister Harold Macmillan and Soviet Premier Nikita Khrushchev.
	May 19–20, 1960	Portugal	Lisbon	Official visit. Met with President Américo Tomás.
16	June 14–16, 1960	Philippines	Manila	State visit. Met with President Carlos P. Garcia.

	June 18–19, 1960	Republic of China	Taipei	State visit. Met with President Chiang Kai-shek.
	June 19–20, 1960	South Korea	Seoul	Met with Prime Minister Heo Jeong. Addressed the National Assembly.
17	October 24, 1960	Mexico	Ciudad Acuña	Informal visit. Met with President Adolfo López Mateos.

Domestic affairs

Modern Republicanism

Eisenhower's approach to politics was described by contemporaries as "modern Republicanism;" modern Republicanism found a middle ground between the liberalism of the New Deal and the conservatism of the Old Guard of the Republican Party.[186] A strong performance in the 1952 elections gave Republicans control of the 83rd United States Congress, though they had narrow majorities in both chambers of Congress. Led by Taft, the conservative faction introduced numerous bills to reduce the federal government's role in American life.[187] Although Eisenhower favored some reduction of the federal government's functions and had strongly opposed President Truman's Fair Deal, he supported the continuation of Social Security and other New Deal programs that he saw as beneficial for the common good.[188] Eisenhower presided over a reduction in domestic spending and reduced the government's role in subsidizing agriculture through passage of the Agricultural Act of 1954,[189] but he did not advocate for the abolition of major New Deal programs such as Social Security or the Tennessee Valley Authority, and these programs remained in place throughout his tenure as president.[190]

Republicans lost control of Congress in the 1954 mid-term elections, and they would not regain control of either chamber until well after Eisenhower left office.[191] Eisenhower's largely nonpartisan stance enabled him to work smoothly with the Speaker of the House Sam Rayburn and Senate Majority Leader Lyndon Johnson.[192] Though liberal members of Congress like Hubert Humphrey and Paul Douglas favored expanding federal aid to education, implementing a national health insurance system, and directing federal assistance to impoverished areas, Rayburn and Johnson largely accepted Eisenhower's relatively conservative domestic policies.[193] In his own party, Eisenhower maintained strong support with moderates, but he frequently clashed with conservative members of Congress, especially over foreign policy.[194] Biographer Jean Edward Smith describes the relationship between Rayburn, Johnson, and Eisenhower: <templatestyles src="Template:Quote/styles.css"/>

> *Ike, LBJ, and "Mr. Sam" did not trust one another completely and they did not see eye to eye on every issue, but they understood one another*

Presidency of Dwight D. Eisenhower 97

Figure 46: *Eisenhower in the Oval Office, February 29, 1956.*

and had no difficulty working together. Eisenhower continued to meet regularly with the Republican leadership. But his weekly sessions with Rayburn and Johnson, usually in the evening, over drinks, were far more productive. For Johnson and Rayburn, it was shrewd politics to cooperate with Ike. Eisenhower was wildly popular in the country....By supporting a Republican president against the Old Guard of his own party, the Democrats hoped to share Ike's popularity.[192]

Fiscal policy and the economy

Federal finances and GDP during Eisenhower's presidency[195]

Year	Income	Outlays	Surplus/ Deficit	GDP	Debt as a % of GDP[196]
1953	69.6	76.1	-6.5	382.5	57.1
1954	69.7	70.9	-1.2	387.7	57.9
1955	65.5	68.4	-3.0	407.0	55.7
1956	74.6	70.6	3.9	439.0	50.6

1957	80.0	76.6	3.4	464.2	47.2
1958	79.6	82.4	-2.8	474.3	47.7
1959	79.2	92.1	-12.8	505.6	46.4
1960	92.5	92.2	0.3	535.1	44.3
1961	94.4	97.8	-3.3	547.6	43.5
Ref.					

Eisenhower was a fiscal conservative whose policy views were close to those of Taft— they agreed that a free enterprise economy should run itself. Throughout Eisenhower's presidency, the top marginal tax rate was 91%—among the highest in American history. When Republicans gained control of both houses of the Congress following the 1952 election, conservatives pressed the president to support tax cuts. Eisenhower however, gave a higher priority to balancing the budget, and believed that taxes could not be cut until it was. "We cannot afford to reduce taxes, [and] reduce income," he said, "until we have in sight a program of expenditure that shows that the factors of income and outgo will be balanced." Eisenhower kept the national debt low and inflation near zero; additionally, three of his eight budgets were in the black.

The 1950s was a period of economic expansion in the United States, and the gross national product jumped from $355.3 billion in 1950 to $487.7 billion in 1960. Unemployment rates were also generally low, expect for in 1958.[197] There were three recessions during Eisenhower's administration—July 1953 through May 1954, August 1957 through April 1958, and April 1960 through February 1961, caused by the Federal Reserve clamping down too tight on the money supply, in an effort to wring out the lingering wartime inflation out of the economy. Meanwhile, federal spending as a percentage of GDP fell from 20.4 to 18.4 percent—there has not been a decline of any size in federal spending as a percentage of GDP during any administration since. Defense spending declined from $50.4 billion in fiscal year 1953 to $40.3 billion in fiscal year 1956, but then rose to $46.6 billion in fiscal year 1959.[198] The stock market performed very well while Eisenhower was in the White House, with the Dow Jones Industrial Average more than doubling (from 288 to 634), and personal income increased by 45 percent. Due to low-cost government loans, the introduction of the credit card, and other factors, total private debt (not including corporations) grew from $104.8 billion in 1950 to $263.3 billion in 1960.[199]

Immigration

At Eisenhower's urging, Congress passed the Refugee Relief Act of 1953, which permitted the admission of 214,000 immigrants to the United States from European countries between 1953 and 1956, over and above existing immigration quotas.[130] The formula for computing the quotas had become more restrictive because of the Immigration and Nationality Act of 1952, approved by Congress over the veto of President Truman. Despite the passage of the Refugee Relief Act, the percentage of foreign-born individuals in the United States continued to drop, reaching 5.4% in 1960. The percentage of native-born individuals with at least one foreign-born parent also reached a new low, at 13.4 percent.[200]

Responding to public outcry, primarily from California, about the perceived costs of services for illegal immigrants from Mexico, the president charged Joseph Swing, Director of the U.S. Immigration and Naturalization Service, with the task of regaining control of the border. On June 17, 1954, Swing launched Operation Wetback, the roundup and deportation of undocumented immigrants in selected areas of California, Arizona, and Texas. The U.S. Border Patrol later reported that over 1.3 million people (a number viewed by many to be inflated and not accurate) were deported or left the U.S. voluntarily under the threat of deportation in 1954. Meanwhile, the number of Mexicans immigrating legally from Mexico grew rapidly during this period, from 18,454 in 1953 to 65,047 in 1956.

Second Red Scare

The onset of the Cold War in the late 1940s had led to a rise in fears of Communist infiltration into the United States. The House established the House Un-American Activities Committee to investigate alleged disloyal activities, while Senator Joseph McCarthy of Wisconsin emerged as a national figure due to his prominence in the anti-Communist movement.[201] Though McCarthy remained a popular figure when Eisenhower took office, his constant attacks on the State Department and the army, and his reckless disregard for due process, offended many inside and outside of Washington, D.C.[202] Privately, Eisenhower held McCarthy and his tactics in contempt, writing, "I despise [McCarthy's tactics], and even during the political campaign of '52 I not only stated publicly (and privately to him) that I disapproved of those methods, but I did so in his own State." Eisenhower's reluctance to publicly oppose McCarthy drew criticism even from many of Eisenhower's own advisers, but the president worked incognito to weaken the popular senator from Wisconsin.[203] In early 1954, after McCarthy escalated his investigation into the army, Eisenhower moved against McCarthy by releasing a report indicating that McCarthy had pressured the army to grant special privileges to an associate, G.

David Schine, who had been drafted.[204] Eisenhower also refused to allow members of the executive branch to testify in the Army–McCarthy hearings, contributing to the collapse of those hearings.[205] Resulting in of the hearings, Senator Ralph Flanders introduced a successful measure to censure McCarthy; Senate Democrats voted unanimously for the censure, while half of the Senate Republicans voted for it. The censure ended McCarthy's status as a major player in national politics, and he died of liver failure in 1957.[206]

Eisenhower disagreed with McCarthy on tactics, but he also considered Communist infiltration to be a serious threat, and he authorized department heads to dismiss employees if there was cause to believe those employees might be disloyal to the United States. Under the direction of Dulles, the State Department purged over 500 employees.[207] With Eisenhower's approval, the Federal Bureau of Investigation (FBI) stepped up domestic surveillance efforts, establishing COINTELPRO in 1956.[208] Eisenhower also declined to commute the sentences of Julius and Ethel Rosenberg, two U.S. citizens who were executed for allegedly providing nuclear secrets to the Soviet Union.[209] In 1957, the Supreme Court handed down a series of decisions that bolstered constitutional protections and curbed the power of the Smith Act. Prosecutions of suspected Communists subsequently declined during the late 1950s.[210]

Civil rights

First term

In the 1950s, African Americans in the South still faced mass disenfranchisement and racially segregated schools, bathrooms, and drinking fountains. Even outside of the South, African Americans faced employment discrimination, housing discrimination, and high rates of poverty and unemployment.[211] Civil rights had emerged as a major national and global issue in the 1940s, partly due to the negative example set by Nazi Germany.[212] Segregation damaged relations with African countries, undercut U.S. calls for decolonization, and emerged as a major theme in Soviet propaganda.[213] Truman had begun the process of desegregating the Armed Forces in 1948, but actual implementation had been slow. Southern Democrats strongly resisted integration, and many Southern leaders had endorsed Eisenhower in 1952 after the latter indicated his opposition to federal efforts to compel integration.[214]

Upon taking office, Eisenhower moved quickly to end resistance to desegregation of the military by using government control of spending to compel compliance from military officials. "Wherever federal funds are expended," he told reporters in March, "I do not see how any American can justify a discrimination in the expenditure of those funds." Later, when Secretary of the Navy Robert B. Anderson stated in a report, "The Navy must recognize the customs and usages prevailing in certain geographic areas of our country which the Navy had no part in creating," Eisenhower responded, "We have not taken and we shall not take a single backward step. There must be no second class citizens in this country."[215] Eisenhower also sought to end discrimination in federal hiring and in Washington, D.C. facilities.[216] Despite these actions, Eisenhower continued to resist becoming involved in the expansion of voting rights, the desegregation of public education, or the eradication of employment discrimination.[212] E. Frederic Morrow, the lone black member of the White House staff, met only occasionally with Eisenhower, and was left with the impression that Eisenhower had little interest in understanding the lives of African Americans.[217]

On May 17, 1954, the Supreme Court handed down its landmark ruling in *Brown v. Board of Education*, declaring state laws establishing separate public schools for black and white students to be unconstitutional. Privately, Eisenhower disapproved of the Supreme Court's holding, stating that he believed it "set back progress in the South at least fifteen years."[218] The president's public response was a frosty, "The Supreme Court has spoken and I am sworn to uphold the constitutional processes in this country; and I will obey." Over the succeeding six years of his presidency, author Robert Caro notes, Eisenhower would never "publicly support the ruling; not once would he say that *Brown* was morally right[.]" His silence left civil rights leaders with the impression that Ike didn't care much about the day-to-day plight of blacks in America, and it served as a source of encouragement for segregationists vowing to resist school desegregation. These segregationists, including the Ku Klux Klan, dealt with a campaign of "massive resistance," violently opposing those who sought to desegregate public education in the South. In 1956, most of Southern members of Congress signed the Southern Manifesto, which called for the overturning of *Brown*.[219]

Second term

As Southern leaders continued to resist desegregation, Eisenhower sought to defuse calls for stronger federal action by introducing a civil rights bill. The bill included provisions designed to increase the protection of African American voting rights; approximately 80% of African Americans were disenfranchised in the mid-1950s.[220] The civil rights bill passed the House relatively easily, but faced strong opposition in the Senate from Southerners, and the bill passed only after many of its original provisions were removed. Though some black leaders urged him to reject the watered-down bill as inadequate, Eisenhower signed the Civil Rights Act of 1957 into law. It was the first federal law designed to protect African Americans since the end of Reconstruction.[221] The act created the United States Commission on Civil Rights and established

Figure 47: *Members of the 327th Airborne Battle Group, 101st Airborne Division, escorting the Little Rock Nine into Little Rock Central High School.*

a civil rights division in the Justice Department, but it also required that defendants in voting rights cases receive a jury trial. The inclusion of the last provision made the act ineffectual, since white jurors in the South would not vote to convict defendants for interfering with the voting rights African Americans.[222]

Eisenhower hoped that the passage of the Civil Rights Act would, at least temporarily, remove the issue of civil rights from the forefront of national politics, but events in Arkansas would force him into action.[223] The school board of Little Rock, Arkansas created a federal court-approved plan for desegregation, with the program to begin implementation at Little Rock Central High School. Fearing that desegregation would complicate his re-election efforts Governor Orval Faubus mobilized the National Guard to prevent nine black students, known as the "Little Rock Nine," from entering Central High. Though Eisenhower had not fully embraced the cause of civil rights, he was determined to uphold federal authority and to prevent an incident that could embarrass the United States on the international stage. Eisenhower convinced Faubus to withdraw the National Guard, but a mob prevented the black students from attending Central High. In response, Eisenhower sent the army into Little Rock, and the army ensured that the Little Rock Nine could attend Central High. Faubus derided Eisenhower's actions, claiming that Little Rock had become "occupied territory," and in 1958 he temporarily shut down Little Rock high schools.[224]

Towards the end of his second term, Eisenhower proposed another civil rights bill designed to help protect voting rights, but Congress once again passed a bill with weaker provisions than Eisenhower had requested. Eisenhower signed the bill into law as the Civil Rights Act of 1960.[225] By 1960, 6.4% of Southern black students attended integrated schools and thousands of black voters had registered to vote, but millions of African Americans remained disenfranchised.[226]

Interstate highway system

Remarks in Cadillac Square, Detroit
President Eisenhower delivered remarks about the need for a new highway program at Cadillac Square in Detroit on October 29, 1954
Text of speech excerpt[227]

Problems playing this file? See media help.

One of Eisenhower's enduring achievements was the Interstate Highway System, which Congress authorized through the Federal Aid Highway Act of 1956. Historian James T. Patterson describes the act as the "only important law" passed during Eisenhower's first term aside from the expansion of Social Security.[228] In 1954, Eisenhower appointed General Lucius D. Clay to head a committee charged with proposing an interstate highway system plan.[229] The president's support for the project was influenced by his experiences as a young army officer crossing the country as part of the 1919 Army Convoy. Summing up motivations for the construction of such a system, Clay stated, <templatestyles src="Template:Quote/styles.css"/>

> *It was evident we needed better highways. We needed them for safety, to accommodate more automobiles. We needed them for defense purposes, if that should ever be necessary. And we needed them for the economy. Not just as a public works measure, but for future growth.*[230,231]

Clay's committee proposed a 10-year, $100 billion program, which would build 40,000 miles of divided highways linking all American cities with a population of greater than 50,000. Eisenhower initially preferred a system consisting of toll roads, but Clay convinced Eisenhower that toll roads were not feasible outside of the highly populated coastal regions. In February 1955, Eisenhower forwarded Clay's proposal to Congress. The bill quickly won approval in the Senate, but House Democrats objected to the use of public bonds as the means to finance construction. Eisenhower and the House Democrats agreed to instead finance the system through the Highway Trust Fund, which itself would be funded by a gasoline tax.[232] Another major infrastructure project,

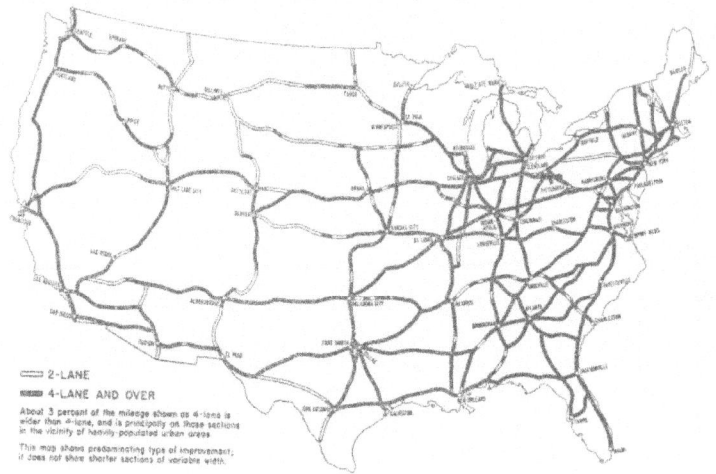

Figure 48: *1955 map: The planned status of U.S Highways in 1965, as a result of the developing Interstate Highway System*

the Saint Lawrence Seaway, was also completed during Eisenhower's presidency.[233]

In long-term perspective the interstate highway system was a remarkable success, that has done much to sustain Eisenhower's positive reputation. Although there have been objections to the negative impact of clearing neighborhoods in cities, the system has been well received. The railroad system for passengers and freight declined sharply, but the trucking expanded dramatically and the cost of shipping and travel fell sharply. Suburbanization became possible, with the rapid growth of easily accessible, larger, cheaper housing than was available in the overcrowded central cities. Tourism dramatically expanded as well, creating a demand for more service stations, motels, restaurants and visitor attractions. There was much more long distance movement to the Sunbelt for winter vacations, or for permanent relocation, with convenient access to visits to relatives back home. In rural areas, towns and small cities off the grid lost out as shoppers followed the interstate, and new factories were located near them.

Space program and education

By 1955, both the U.S. and the U.S.S.R. were building ballistic missiles that could be utilized to launch objects into space. That year, in separate announcements four days apart, both nations publicly announced that they would launch artificial Earth satellites within the next few years. The July 29, announcement from the White House stated that the U.S. would launch "small Earth circling satellites" between July 1, 1957, and December 31, 1958, as part of the American contribution to the International Geophysical Year.[234] Americans were astonished when October 4, 1957, the Soviet Union launched its *Sputnik 1* satellite into orbit Three months later, a nationally televised test of the American Vanguard TV3 missile failed in an embarrassing fashion; the missile was facetiously referred to as "Flopnik" and "Stay-putnik."[235]

To many, the success of the Soviet satellite program suggested that the Soviet Union had made a substantial leap forward in technology that posed a serious threat to U.S. national security. While Eisenhower initially downplayed the gravity of the Soviet launch, public fear and anxiety about the perceived technological gap grew. Americans rushed to build nuclear bomb shelters, while the Soviet Union boasted about its new superiority as a world power. The president was, as British prime minister Harold Macmillan observed during a June 1958 visit to the U.S., "under severe attack for the first time" in his presidency.[236] Economist Bernard Baruch wrote in an open letter to the *New York Herald Tribune* titled "The Lessons of Defeat": "While we devote our industrial and technological power to producing new model automobiles and more gadgets, the Soviet Union is conquering space. ... It is Russia, not the United States, who has had the imagination to hitch its wagon to the stars and the skill to reach for the moon and all but grasp it. America is worried. It should be."

The launch spurred a series of federal government initiatives ranging from defense to education. Renewed emphasis was placed on the Explorers program (which had earlier been supplanted by Project Vanguard) to launch an American satellite into orbit; this was accomplished on January 31, 1958 with the successful launch of Explorer 1.[237] In February 1958, Eisenhower authorized formation of the Advanced Research Projects Agency, later renamed the Defense Advanced Research Projects Agency (DARPA), within the Department of Defense to develop emerging technologies for the U.S. military. On July 29, 1958, he signed the National Aeronautics and Space Act, which established NASA as a civilian space agency. NASA as created by Congress was substantially stronger than the administration's original proposal. NASA took over the space technology research started by DARPA, as well as the air force's manned satellite program, Man In Space Soonest, which was renamed as Project Mercury. The project's first seven astronauts were announced on April 9, 1959.

In September 1958, the president signed into law the National Defense Education Act, a four-year program that poured billions of dollars into the U.S. education system. In 1953 the government spent $153 million, and colleges took $10 million of that funding; however, by 1960 the combined funding grew almost six-fold as a result. Meanwhile, during the late 1950s and into the 1960s, NASA, the Department of Defensed, and various private sector corporationsdeveloped multiple communications satellite research and development programs.

Labor unions

Union membership peaked in the mid-1950s, when unions consisting of about one-quarter of the total work force. The Congress of Industrial Organizations and the American Federation of Labor merged in 1955 to form the AFL–CIO, the largest federation of unions in the United States. Unlike some of his predecessors, AFL–CIO leader George Meany did not emphasize organizing unskilled workers and workers in the South.[238] During the late 1940s and the 1950s, both the business community and local Republicans wanted to weaken unions, which played a major role in funding and campaigning for Democratic candidates.[239] The Eisenhower administration also worked to consolidate the anti-union potential inherent in Taft–Hartley Act of 1947. Republicans sought to delegitimize unions by focusing on their shady activities, and the Justice Department, the Labor Department, and Congress all conducted investigations of criminal activity and racketeering in high-profile labor unions, especially the Teamsters Union. A select Senate committee, the McClellan Committee, was created in January 1957, and its hearings targeted Teamsters Union president James R. Hoffa as a public enemy.[240] Public opinion polls showed growing distrust toward unions, and especially union leaders—or "labor bosses," as Republicans called them. The bipartisan Conservative Coalition, with liberals such as the Kennedy brothers, won new congressional restrictions on organized labor in the 1959 Landrum-Griffin Act. The main impact of that act was to force more democracy on the previously authoritarian union hierarchies.[241] However, in the 1958 elections, the unions fought back against state right-to-work laws and defeated many conservative Republicans.

Mid-term elections of 1958

The economy began to decline in mid-1957 and reached its nadir in early 1958. The Recession of 1958 was the worst economic downturn of Eisenhower's tenure, as the unemployment rate reached a high of 7.5%. The poor economy, *Sputnik*, the federal intervention in Little Rock, and a contentious budget battle all sapped Eisenhower's popularity, with Gallup polling showing that his approval rating dropped from 79 percent in February 1957 to 52 percent in March 1958.[242] A controversy broke out in mid-1958 after a House subcommittee discovered that White House Chief of Staff Sherman Adams had accepted an expensive gift from Bernard Goldfine, textile manufacturer under investigation by the Federal Trade Commission (FTC). Adams denied the accusation that he had interfered with the FTC investigation on Goldfine's behalf, but Eisenhower forced him to resign in September 1958.[243] In the 1958 mid-term elections, the Democrats attacked Eisenhower over the Space Race, the controversy relating to Adams, and other issues, but the biggest issue of the campaign was the economy, which had not yet fully recovered. Republicans suffered major defeats in the 1958 mid-term elections, since Democrats picked up over forty seats in the House and over ten seats in the Senate. Several leading Republicans, including Bricker and Senate Minority Leader William Knowland, lost their re-election campaigns.[244]

Twenty-third Amendment

Under the original constitutional rules governing the Electoral College, presidential electors were apportioned to states only. As a result, the District of Columbia was excluded from the presidential election process. Several constitutional amendments to provide the district's citizens with appropriate rights of voting in national elections for president and vice president were introduced in Congress during the 1950s. Eisenhower was a persistent advocate for the voting rights of D.C. residents.[245] On June 16, 1960, the 86th Congress approved a constitutional amendment extending the right to vote in presidential election to citizens residing in the District of Columbia by granting the district electors in the Electoral College, as if it were a state. After the requisite number state legislatures ratified the proposed amendment, it became the Twenty-third Amendment to the United States Constitution on March 29, 1961.

States admitted to the Union

Eisenhower had called for the admission of Alaska and Hawaii as states during his 1952 campaign. However, various issues delayed their statehood. Hawaii faced opposition from Southern members of Congress who objected to the island chain's large non-white population, while concerns about military bases in Alaska convinced Eisenhower to oppose statehood for the territory early in his tenure.[246] In 1958, Eisenhower reached an agreement with Congress on a bill that provided for the admission of Alaska and set aside large portions of Alaska for military bases. Eisenhower signed the Alaska Statehood Act into law in July 1958, and Alaska became the 49th state on January 3, 1959. Two months later, Eisenhower signed the Hawaii Admission Act, and Hawaii became the 50th state in August 1959.[247]

Figure 49: *The states of the United States in August 1959*

Health issues

Eisenhower began chain smoking cigarettes at West Point. He stopped in 1949. He was the first president to release information about his health and medical records while in office. However people around him covered up medical information that might hurt him politically by raising doubts about his good health. On September 24, 1955, while vacationing in Colorado, he had a serious heart attack.[248] Dr. Howard Snyder, his personal physician, misdiagnosed the symptoms as indigestion, and failed to call in the help that was urgently needed. Snyder later falsified his own records to cover his blunder and to protect Eisenhower's need to portray he was healthy enough to do his job.[249,250,251] The heart attack required six weeks' hospitalization, and Eisenhower did not resume his normal work schedule until early 1956. During Eisenhower's period of recuperation, Nixon, Dulles, and Sherman Adams assumed administrative duties and provided communication with the president.[252] Eisenhower suffered a stroke in November 1957, but he quickly recovered.[253] His health was generally good for the remainder of his second term.[254]

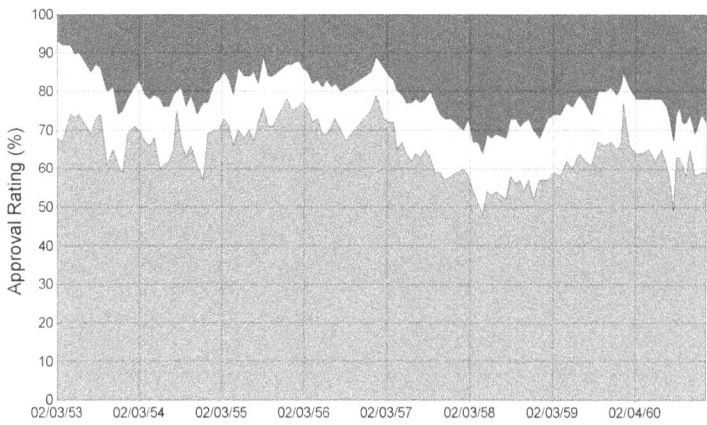

Figure 50: *Graph of Eisenhower's Gallup approval ratings*

Presidential elections

1956 re-election

In July 1955, *TIME* Magazine lauded the president for bringing "prosperity to the nation," noting that, "In the 29 months since Dwight Eisenhower moved into the White House, a remarkable changes has come over the nation. Blood pressure and temperature have gone down; nerve endings have healed over. The new tone could be described in a word: confidence." As the country had been enjoying a period of relative prosperity and confidence during Eisenhower's first term, and as his Gallup poll approval rating ranged between 68 and 79 percent, few doubted that he would be reelected in 1956. Eisenhower's September 1955 heart attack engendered speculation about whether he would be able to seek a second term. However, after his doctor pronounced him fully recovered in February 1956, Eisenhower announced his decision to run for re-election. Eisenhower had considered retiring after one term, but decided to run again in part because he viewed his potential successors from both parties as inadequate.[255]

Eisenhower did not trust Nixon to ably lead the country if he acceded to the presidency, and he attempted to remove Nixon from the 1956 ticket by offering him the position of Secretary of Defense. Nixon declined the offer, and refused to take his name out of consideration for re-nomination unless Eisenhower demanded it. Unwilling to split the party, and unable to find the perfect replacement for Nixon, Eisenhower decided not to oppose Nixon's re-nomination.[256] Some in the party continued to oppose Nixon, including

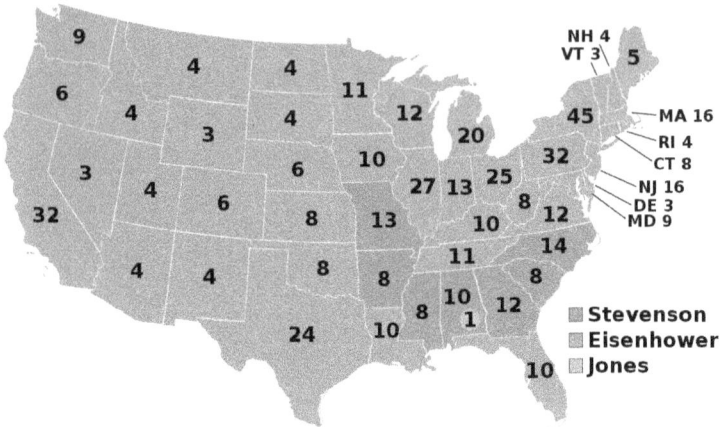

Figure 51: *1956 electoral vote results*

Harold Stassen, who worked in vain, through to the convention, to coax someone to come forward and challenge Nixon. Nixon remained highly popular among the Republican leadership and rank-and-file voters, and the vice president was unanimously re-nominated at the 1956 Republican National Convention. Eisenhower, meanwhile, was renominated with no opposition.

At the 1956 Democratic National Convention in Chicago, Illinois, Adlai Stevenson was renominated on the first ballot, despite a strong challenge from New York governor W. Averell Harriman, who was backed by former president Truman.[257] Stevenson announced that he would leave the choice of the candidate for vice president to the convention; he gave no indication of who he would prefer to have for a running mate. Delegates chose Senator Estes Kefauver of Tennessee on the second ballot.

Eisenhower campaigned on his record of economic prosperity and his Cold War foreign policy.[258] He also attacked Democrats for allegedly blocking his legislative programs and derided Stevenson's proposal to ban the testing of nuclear weapons.[259] Stevenson called for an acceleration of disarmament talks with the Soviet Union and increased government spending on social programs.Wikipedia:Citation needed Democrats introduced the tactic of negative television ads, generally attacking Nixon rather than Eisenhower.[260] The Suez Crisis and the Hungarian Revolution became the focus of Eisenhower's attention in the final weeks of the campaign, and his actions in the former crises boosted his popularity.[261]

On election day, Eisenhower won by an even greater margin than he had four years earlier, taking 457 electoral votes to Stevenson's 73.[257] He won over

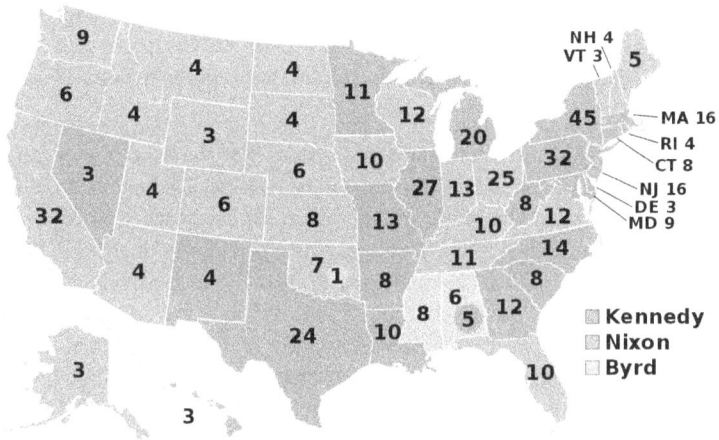

Figure 52: *1960 electoral vote results*

57 percent of the popular vote, taking over 35 million votes.[262] Eisenhower maintained his 1952 gains among Democrats, especially white urban Southerners and Northern Catholics, while the growing suburbs added to his Republican base. Compared to the 1952 election, Eisenhower gained Kentucky, Louisiana, and West Virginia, while losing Missouri. In interviews with pollsters, his voters were less likely to bring up his leadership record. Instead what stood out this time, "was the response to personal qualities— to his sincerity, his integrity and sense of duty, his virtue as a family man, his religious devotion, and his sheer likeableness." Eisenhower's victory did not provide a strong coattail effect for other Republican candidates, and Democrats retained control of Congress.[263]

1960 election and transition

The 22nd Amendment to the U.S. Constitution, ratified in 1951, established a two-term limit for the presidency. As the amendment had not applied to President Truman, Eisenhower became the first president constitutionally limited to two terms. Eisenhower nonetheless closely watched the 1960 presidential election, which he viewed as a referendum on his presidency. He attempted to convince Secretary of the Treasury Robert Anderson to seek the Republican nomination, but Anderson declined to enter the race.[264] Eisenhower offered Nixon lukewarm support in the 1960 Republican primaries. When asked by reporters to list one of Nixon's policy ideas he had adopted, Eisenhower joked, "If you give me a week, I might think of one. I don't remember." Eisenhower and Nixon in fact had become unequal friends, who learned it from each other and respected each other.[265] Despite the lack of strong support from Eisenhower, Nixon's successful cultivation of party elites ensured that he faced only a weak challenge from Governor Nelson Rockefeller for the Republican nomination.[266]

The 1960 campaign was dominated by the Cold War and the economy. John F. Kennedy triumphed at the 1960 Democratic National Convention, defeating Lyndon B. Johnson, Hubert Humphrey, and other candidates to become the party's presidential nominee. To shore up support in the South and West, Kennedy chose Johnson as his running mate. In the general election, Kennedy attacked the alleged "missile gap" and endorsed federal aid for education, an increased minimum wage, and the establishment of a federal health insurance program for the elderly.[267] Nixon, meanwhile, wanted to win on his own, and did not take up Eisenhower's offers for help.[268] To Eisenhower's great disappointment, Kennedy defeated Nixon in an extremely close election.[269] Kennedy took 49.7 percent of the popular vote and won the electoral vote by a margin of 303-to-219.[270]

During the campaign, Eisenhower had privately lambasted Kennedy's inexperience and connections to political machines, but after the election he worked with Kennedy to ensure a smooth transition. He personally met twice with Kennedy, emphasizing especially the danger posed by Cuba.[271] On January 17, 1961, Eisenhower gave his final televised Address to the Nation from the Oval Office. In his farewell address, Eisenhower raised the issue of the Cold War and role of the U.S. armed forces. He described the Cold War: "We face a hostile ideology global in scope, atheistic in character, ruthless in purpose and insidious in method ..." and warned about what he saw as unjustified government spending proposals and continued with a warning that "we must guard against the acquisition of unwarranted influence, whether sought or unsought, by the military–industrial complex." Eisenhower's address reflected his fear that military spending and the desire to ensure total security would be pursued to the detriment of other goals, including a sound economy, efficient social programs, and individual liberties.[272]

Historical reputation

Eisenhower was popular among the general public when he left office, but for a decade or two commentators viewed Eisenhower as a "do-nothing" president who left many of the major decisions to his subordinates. Paul Holbo and Robert W. Sellen state that critics portrayed Eisenhower:

> typically with a golf club in his hand and a broad but vapid grin on his face....liberal intellectuals compared him unfavorably with their standard for president, Franklin D. Roosevelt. They gave "Ike" especially low

marks For his seeming aloofness from politics, his refusal to battle publicly with Senator Joseph McCarthy, and his reluctance to assume active party leadership.[273]

However, the study of previously-closed records and papers showed that Eisenhower shrewdly maneuvered behind the scenes, avoiding controversial issues while retaining control of his administration. Historians have also noted the limits of some of Eisenhower's achievements; he avoided taking strong public stances on McCarthyism or civil rights, and Cold War tensions were high at the end of his presidency. Recent polls of historians and political scientists have generally ranked Eisenhower in the top quartile of presidents. A 2018 poll of the American Political Science Association's Presidents and Executive Politics section ranked Eisenhower as the seventh best president. A 2017 C-Span poll of historians ranked Eisenhower as the fifth best president.

Historian John Lewis Gaddis has summarized the turnaround in evaluations:

Historians long ago abandoned the view that Eisenhower's was a failed presidency. He did, after all, end the Korean War without getting into any others. He stabilized, and did not escalate, the Soviet-American rivalry. He strengthened European alliances while withdrawing support from European colonialism. He rescued the Republican Party from isolationism and McCarthyism. He maintained prosperity, balanced the budget, promoted technological innovation, facilitated (if reluctantly) the civil rights movement and warned, in the most memorable farewell address since Washington's, of a "military–industrial complex" that could endanger the nation's liberties. Not until Reagan would another president leave office with so strong a sense of having accomplished what he set out to do.[274]

References

Works cited

- Ambrose, Stephen E. (1983). *Eisenhower*. Volume I: Soldier, General of the Army, President-Elect, 1890-1952. Simon and Schuster. ISBN 0671440691.
- Ambrose, Stephen E. (1984). *Eisenhower*. Volume II: President and Elder Statesman, 1952-1969. Simon and Schuster. ISBN 0671605658.
- Kabaservice, Geoffrey (2012). *Rule and Ruin: The Downfall of Moderation and the Destruction of the Republican Party, from Eisenhower to the Tea Party*. Oxford University Press. ISBN 9780199768400.
- Lyon, Peter (1974). *Eisenhower: Portrait of the Hero*. Little Brown and Company. ISBN 0316540218.

- Morison, Samuel Eliot (1965). *The Oxford History of the American People*. New York: Oxford University Press. LCCN 65-12468[275].
- Pach, Chester J.; Richardson, Elmo (1991). *The Presidency of Dwight D. Eisenhower* (Revised ed.). University Press of Kansas. ISBN 0-7006-0437-5.
- Patterson, James (1996). *Grand Expectations: The United States 19451974*. Oxford University Press. ISBN 978-0195117974.
- Pusey, Merlo J. (1956). *Eisenhower The President*[276]. Macmillan. LCCN 56-8365[277].
- Schefter, James (1999). *The Race: The uncensored story of how America beat Russia to the Moon*[278]. New York: Doubleday. ISBN 0-385-49253-7.
- Smith, Jean Edward (2012). *Eisenhower in War and Peace*[279]. Random House. ISBN 978-1400066933.
- Wicker, Tom (2002). *Dwight D. Eisenhower*. Times Books. ISBN 0-8050-6907-0.

Further reading

Biographies

- Ambrose, Stephen E. *Eisenhower: Soldier and President* (2003). A revision and condensation of his earlier two-volume Eisenhower biography.
- Gellman, Irwin F. *The President and the Apprentice: Eisenhower and Nixon, 1952–1961* (2015).
- Krieg, Joann P. ed. *Dwight D. Eisenhower, Soldier, President, Statesman* (1987). 24 essays by scholars.
- Mayer, Michael S. *The Eisenhower Years* (2009), 1024pp; short biographies by experts of 500 prominent figures, with some primary sources.
- Newton, Jim, *Eisenhower: The White House Years* (Random House, 2011) online[280]
- Nichols, David A. *Eisenhower 1956: The President's Year of Crisis–Suez and the Brink of War* (2012).
- Schoenebaum, Eleanora, ed. *Political Profiles the Eisenhower Years* (1977); 757pp; short political biographies of 501 major players in politics in the 1950s.

Scholarly studies

- Anderson J. W. *Eisenhower, Brownell, and the Congress: The Tangled Origins of the Civil Rights Bill of 1956–1957*. University of Alabama Press, 1964.

- Bean Louis, *Influences in the 1954 Mid-Term Elections.* Washington: Public Affairs Institute, 1954
- Burns James MacGregor, *The Deadlock of Democracy.* Prentice-Hall, 1963
- Burrows, William E. *This New Ocean: The Story of the First Space Age.* New York: Random House, 1998. 282pp
- Congressional Quarterly. *Congress and the Nation 1945–1964* (1965), Highly detailed and factual coverage of Congress and presidential politics; 1784 pages
- Corwin Edward S., and Koenig Louis W. *The Presidency Today.* New York University Press, 1956.
- Damms, Richard V. *The Eisenhower Presidency, 1953–1961* (2002)
- David Paul T. (ed.), *Presidential Nominating Politics in 1952.* 5 vols., Johns Hopkins Press, 1954.
- Eulau Heinz, *Class and Party in the Eisenhower Years.* Free Press, 1962. voting behavior
- Greene, John Robert. *I Like Ike: The Presidential Election of 1952* (2017) excerpt[281]
- Greenstein, Fred I. *The Hidden-Hand Presidency: Eisenhower as Leader* (1991).
- Harris, Douglas B. "Dwight Eisenhower and the New Deal: The Politics of Preemption" *Presidential Studies Quarterly,* 27#2 (1997) pp 333–41 in JSTOR[282].
- Harris, Seymour E. *The Economics of the Political Parties, with Special Attention to Presidents Eisenhower and Kennedy* (1962)
- Holbo, Paul S. and Robert W. Sellen, eds. *The Eisenhower era: the age of consensus* (1974), 196pp; 20 short excerpts from primary and secondary sources online[283]
- Kaufman, Burton I. and Diane Kaufman. *Historical Dictionary of the Eisenhower Era* (2009), 320pp
- Medhurst; Martin J. *Dwight D. Eisenhower: Strategic Communicator* (Greenwood Press, 1993).
- Nichols, David A. *Ike and McCarthy: Dwight Eisenhower's Secret Campaign against Joseph McCarthy* (2017). excerpt[284]
- Olson, James S. *Historical Dictionary of the 1950s* (2000)
- Pach, Chester J. ed. *A Companion to Dwight D. Eisenhower* (2017), new essays by experts; stress on historiography.
- Pickett, William B. (1995). *Dwight David Eisenhower and American Power.* Wheeling, Ill.: Harlan Davidson. ISBN 0-88-295918-2. OCLC 31206927[285].
- Pickett, William B. (2000). *Eisenhower Decides to Run: Presidential Politics and Cold War Strategy.* Chicago: Ivan R. Dee. ISBN 1-56-

663787-2. OCLC 43953970[286].
- Wayne, Stephen J. "The Eisenhower Administration: Bridge to the Institutionalized Legislative Presidency." Congress & the Presidency. 39#2 (2012).

Foreign and military policy

- Bose, Meenekshi. *Shaping and signaling presidential policy: The national security decision making of Eisenhower and Kennedy* (Texas A&M UP, 1998).
- Bowie, Robert R. and Richard H. Immerman, eds. *Waging peace: how Eisenhower shaped an enduring cold war strategy* (1998) online[287]
- Brands, Henry W. *Cold Warriors: Eisenhower's Generation and American Foreign Policy* (Columbia UP, 1988).
- Broadwater; Jeff. *Eisenhower & the Anti-Communist Crusade* (U of North Carolina Press, 1992) online at Questia[288].
- Bury, Helen. *Eisenhower and the Cold War arms race:'Open Skies' and the military-industrial complex* (2014).
- Caridi Ronald J., *The Korean War and American Politics.* (U of Pennsylvania Press, 1968).
- Chernus, Ira. *Apocalypse Management: Eisenhower and the Discourse of National Insecurity.* (Stanford UP, 2008).
- Divine, Robert A. *Eisenhower and the Cold War* (1981)
- Divine, Robert A. *Foreign Policy and U.S. Presidential Elections, 1952–1960* (1974).
- Herring, George C. (2008). *From Colony to Superpower; U.S. Foreign Relations Since 1776.* Oxford University Press. ISBN 978-0-19-507822-0.
- Jackson, Michael Gordon (2005). "Beyond Brinkmanship: Eisenhower, Nuclear War Fighting, and Korea, 1953-1968". *Presidential Studies Quarterly.* **35** (1): 52–75. doi: 10.1111/j.1741-5705.2004.00235.x[289].
- Jones, Matthew (2008). "Targeting China: US nuclear planning and "massive retaliation" in East Asia, 1953–1955". *Journal of Cold War Studies.* **10** (4): 37–65. doi: 10.1162/jcws.2008.10.4.37[290].
- Matray, James I (2011). "Korea's war at 60: A survey of the literature". *Cold War History.* **11** (1): 99–129. doi: 10.1080/14682745.2011.545603[291].
- Melanson, Richard A. and David A. Mayers, eds. *Reevaluating Eisenhower: American foreign policy in the 1950s* (1989) online[292]
- Osgood, Kenneth. *Total Cold War: Eisenhower's Secret Propaganda Battle at Home and Abroad.* (U of Kansas Press, 2006).

- Rosenberg, Victor. *Soviet-American relations, 1953–1960: diplomacy and cultural exchange during the Eisenhower presidency* (McFarland, 2005).
- Watry, David M. *Diplomacy at the Brink: Eisenhower, Churchill, and Eden in the Cold War* (LSU Press, 2014).

Primary sources

- Adams, Sherman. *Firsthand Report: The Story of the Eisenhower Administration.* 1961. by Ike's chief of staff
- Benson, Ezra Taft. *Cross Fire: The Eight Years with Eisenhower* (1962) Secretary of Agriculture online at Questia[293]
- Peter G. Boyle, ed. *The Churchill-Eisenhower Correspondence, 1953–1955* (U North Carolina Press, 1990). online at Questia[294]
- Brownell, Herbert and John P. Burke. *Advising Ike: The Memoirs of Attorney General Herbert Brownell* (1993).
- Eisenhower, Dwight D. *Mandate for Change, 1953–1956*, Doubleday and Co., 1963; his memoir
- Eisenhower, Dwight D. *The White House Years: Waging Peace 1956–1961*, Doubleday and Co., 1965; his memoir
- *Papers of Dwight D. Eisenhower* The 21 volume Johns Hopkins print edition of Eisenhower's papers includes: *The Presidency: The Middle Way* (vols. 14–17) and *The Presidency: Keeping the Peace* (vols. 18-21), his private letters and papers online at subscribing libraries[295]
- Eisenhower, Dwight D. *Public Papers*, covers 1953 through end of term in 1961. based on White House press releases online[296]
- Gallup, George H., ed. *The Gallup Poll: Public Opinion, 1935–1971.* (3 vols. Random House, 1972). press releases summarizing all their polls
- Hagerty, James C. *The Diary of James C. Hagerty: Eisenhower in Mid-Course, 1954–1955*. Edited by Robert H. Ferrell. (Indiana UP, 1983). by the press secretary
- Hughes, Emmet John. *The Ordeal of Power: A Political Memoir of the Eisenhower Years.* 1963. Ike's speechwriter
- Lodge, Henry Cabot. *As It Was: An Inside View of Politics and Power in the '50s and '60s* 1976, ambassador to UN
- Martin, Joe. *My First Fifty Years in Politics* 1960. House GOP leader
- Nixon, Richard M. *The Memoirs of Richard Nixon* 1978.
- Howard Nathaniel R. ed., *The Basic Papers of George M. Humphrey as Secretary of the Treasury, 1913–1957* (The Western Reserve Historical Society, 1965).
- Logsdon, John M., Linda J. Lear, and Roger D. Launius. "II-15." Exploring the Unknown: Selected Documents in the History of the U.S. Civil Space Program. Washington, D.C.: NASA, 1995. 331-363.

- *Documentary History of the Dwight D. Eisenhower Presidency* (13 vol. University Publications of America, 1996) online table of contents[297]

External links
- Papers and Records of President Dwight D. Eisenhower, Dwight D. Eisenhower Presidential Library[298]

Appendix

References

[1] //en.wikipedia.org/w/index.php?title=Template:Eisenhower_series&action=edit
[2] Quirk, Robert E. (1993). Fidel Castro. p. 303 New York and London: W.W. Norton & Company.
[3] D'Este, Carlo (2002). *Eisenhower: A Soldier's Life*, p. 25.
[4] Bergman, Jerry. "Steeped in Religion: President Eisenhower and the Influence of the Jehovah's Witnesses", *Kansas History* (Autumn 1998).
[5] D'Este, Carlo (2002). *Eisenhower: A Soldier's Life*, p. 58.
[6] online "Faith Staked Down" http://www.time.com/time/magazine/article/0,9171,889614,00.html, *Time*, February 9, 1953.
[7]
[8] Owen, David (1999). *The Making of the Masters: Clifford Roberts, Augusta National, and Golf's Most Prestigious Tournament*, Simon and Schuster, .
[9] Ambrose (1983), p.56.
[10] Ambrose (1983), p.62.
[11] American President: An Online Reference Resource, *Dwight David Eisenhower (1890–1969)*, "Life Before the Presidency," http://millercenter.org/president/eisenhower/essays/biography/2 Miller Center of Public Affairs, University of Virginia.
[12] Irish, Kerry. "Dwight Eisenhower and Douglas MacArthur in the Philippines: There Must Be a Day of Reckoning", *Journal of Military History*, April 2010, Vol. 74, Issue 2, pp. 439–73.
[13] Korda (2007), pp 239–243
[14] Eisenhower lived in 'Telegraph Cottage', Warren Road, Coombe, Kingston upon Thames from 1942 to 1944. In 1995, a plaque commemorating this was placed there by the Royal Borough of Kingston upon Thames. It can be seen at the north end of Warren Road.
[15] Atkinson, *An Army at Dawn*, pp. 251–2.
[16] Ambrose (1983), pp. 230–3.
[17] William Safire, *Lend me your ears: great speeches in history* (2004) p. 1143
[18] Jean Edward Smith, *Eisenhower in War and Peace* (2012) p. 451.
[19] Zink, Harold (1947). *American Military Government in Germany*, pp. 39–86
[20] Goedde, Petra. "From Villains to Victims: Fraternization and the Feminization of Germany, 1945–1947", *Diplomatic History*, Winter 1999, Vol. 23, Issue 1, pp. 1–19
[21] Tent, James F. (1982), *Mission on the Rhine: Reeducation and Denazification in American-Occupied Germany*
[22] Zink, Harold (1957). *The United States in Germany, 1944–1955*
[23] Ambrose (1983). *Eisenhower*, pp. 421–5
[24] Goedde, Petra (2002). *GIs and Germans: Culture, Gender and Foreign Relations, 1945–1949*
[25] Richard Rhodes, *The Making of the Atomic Bomb*, with Rhodes citing a 1963 profile called "Ike on Ike, in *Newsweek* November 11, 1963
[26] " Truman Wrote of '48 Offer to Eisenhower https://www.nytimes.com/2003/07/11/us/truman-wrote-of-48-offer-to-eisenhower.html?fta=y" *The New York Times*, July 11, 2003.
[27] Ambrose (1983). *Eisenhower*, ch. 24
[28] *Crusade in Europe*, Doubleday; 1st edition (1948), 559 pages,
[29] Pietrusza, David, 1948: Harry Truman's Victory and the Year That Transformed America, Union Square Punlishing, 2011, p. 201
[30] Warshaw, Shirley Anne (1993). *Reexamining the Eisenhower presidency*, Greenwood Press,
[31] Ambrose (1983). *Eisenhower*, pp. 556–67.
[32] http://www.fhwa.dot.gov/interstate/audiotext.htm#cadillac
[33] Eisenhower, Susan, "50 years later, we're still ignoring Ike's warning" https://www.washingtonpost.com/wp-dyn/content/article/2011/01/14/AR2011011404915.html, *The Washington Post*, January 16, 2011, p. B3.

[34] Greenberg, David (January 14, 2011) "Beware the military–industrial Complex" https://web.archive.org/web/20110119121008/http://www.slate.com/id/2281124/pagenum/all/, *Slate*
[35] John M. Logsdon, "Exploring the Unknown: Selected Documents in the History of the U.S. Civil Space Program" (NASA; 1995)
[36] Logsdon, John M, and Lear, Linda J. Exploring the Unknown:Selected Documents in the History of the U.S. Civil Space Program/ Washington D.C.
[37] W. D. Kay, Defining NASA The Historical Debate Over the Agency's Mission, 2005.
[38] Parmet, Herbert S. Eisenhower and the American Crusades (New York: The Macmillan Company, 1972)
[39] Yankek Mieczkowski, *Eisenhower's Sputnik Moment: The Race for Space and World Prestige* (Cornell University Press; 2013)
[40] Peter J. Roman, *Eisenhower and the Missile Gap* (1996)
[41] The Presidents's Science Advisory Committee, "Report of the Ad Hoc Panel on Man-in-Space" December 16, 1960. NASA Historical Collection
[42] Greg Ward, "A Rough Guide History of the USA" (Penguin Group: London, 2003)
[43] Ambrose (1984), p. 106-7
[44] Eisenhower gave verbal approval to Secretary of State John Foster Dulles and to Director of Central Intelligence Allen Dulles to proceed with the coup; Ambrose, *Eisenhower, Vol. 2: The President* p. 111; Ambrose (1990), *Eisenhower: Soldier and President*, New York: Simon and Schuster, p. 333
[45] Kingseed, Cole (1995), *Eisenhower and the Suez Crisis of 1956*, ch 6
[46] Dwight D. Eisenhower, *Waging Peace: 1956–1961* (1965) p 99
[47] Isaac Alteras, *Eisenhower and Israel: U.S.–Israeli Relations, 1953–1960* (1993), p. 296
[48] Dunnigan, James and Nofi, Albert (1999), *Dirty Little Secrets of the Vietnam War*. St. Martins Press, p. 85.
[49] Dunnigan, James and Nofi, Albert (1999), *Dirty Little Secrets of the Vietnam War*, p. 257
[50] Karnow, Stanley. (1991), *Vietnam, A History*, p. 230
[51] Reeves, Richard (1993), *President Kennedy: Profile of Power*, p. 75
[52] Bogle, Lori Lynn, ed. (2001), The Cold War, Routledge, p. 104. 978-0815337218
[53] State of the Union Address, February 2, 1953, Public Papers, 1953 pp. 30–1.
[54] Byrnes to DDE, August 27, 1953, Eisenhower Library"
[55] Dudziak, Mary L. (2002), *Cold War Civil Rights: Race and the Image of American Democracy*
[56] to DDE, September 25, 1957, Eisenhower Library
[57] Joseph W. Martin as told to Donavan, Robert J. (1960), *My First Fifty Years in Politics*, New York: McGraw Hill, p. 227
[58] Newton, *Eisenhower* (2011) pp. 356-7
[59] Newton, *Eisenhower* pp 196–199.
[60] Clarence G. Lasby, *Eisenhower's Heart Attack: How Ike Beat Heart Disease and Held on to the Presidency* (1997) pp. 57–113.
[61] Robert P. Hudson, "Eisenhower's Heart Attack: How Ike Beat Heart Disease and Held on to the Presidency (review)" *Bulletin of the History of Medicine* 72#1 (1998) pp. 161–162 online https://muse.jhu.edu/article/4010.
[62] R.H. Ferrell, 'Ill-Advised: Presidential Health & Public Trust *(1992), pp. 53–150*
[63] Williams, Charles *Harold Macmillan* (2009) p. 345
[64] Messerli F. H., Loughlin K. R., Messerli A. W., Welch W. R.: The President and the pheochromocytoma. *Am J Cardiol* 2007; 99: 1325–1329.
[65] Nixon, Richard, The Memoirs of Richard Nixon, 1978, pp. 222-3.
[66] *Post Presidential Years* http://eisenhower.archives.gov/All_About_Ike/Post_Presidential/Post_Presidential.html. Eisenhower Archives. "President Kennedy reactivated his commission as a five star general in the United States Army. With the exception of George Washington, Eisenhower is the only United States President with military service to reenter the Armed Forces after leaving the office of President."
[67] John Lewis Gaddis, "He Made It Look Easy: 'Eisenhower in War and Peace', by Jean Edward Smith" https://www.nytimes.com/2012/04/22/books/review/eisenhower-in-war-and-peace-by-jean-edward-smith.html?_r=1&pagewanted=all, *New York Times Book Review*, April 20, 2012.

[68] Morgenthau, Hans J.: "Goldwater – The Romantic Regression", in *Commentary*, September 1964.
[69] This law allowed only 75% of pay and allowances to the grade for those on the retired list.
[70] The retirement provisions were also applied to the World War II Commandant of the Marine Corps and the Commandant of the Coast Guard, both of whom held four-star rank.
[71] Prince Bernhard of the Netherlands in an interview with H.G. Meijer, published in "Het Vliegerkruis", Amsterdam 1997, . p. 92.
[72] Finding aid for the Metropolitan Museum of Art 75th Anniversary Committee records, 1945–1950 http://libmma.org/digital_files/archives/Met_Museum_75th_Anniversary_Committee_records_b18084369.pdf, Metropolitan Museum of Art.
[73] //www.worldcat.org/oclc/55665502
[74] //www.worldcat.org/oclc/482017
[75] //www.worldcat.org/oclc/49893871
[76] https://www.amazon.com/Supreme-Commander-Years-Dwight-Eisenhower/dp/0307946622/
[77] https://books.google.com/books?id=ag7omy2OvBgC
[78] //www.worldcat.org/oclc/617565184
[79] //www.worldcat.org/oclc/892458610
[80] //www.worldcat.org/oclc/1247005
[81] //www.worldcat.org/oclc/6863111
[82] //www.worldcat.org/oclc/105454244
[83] https://www.worldcat.org/oclc/519846
[84] https://www.worldcat.org/oclc/910504324
[85] https://www.worldcat.org/oclc/8765635
[86] https://www.worldcat.org/oclc/174566
[87] https://www.worldcat.org/oclc/26764309
[88] https://www.worldcat.org/oclc/694394274
[89] https://www.worldcat.org/oclc/22307949
[90] //www.worldcat.org/oclc/43953970
[91] //www.worldcat.org/oclc/31206927
[92] https://www.jstor.org/stable/1901942
[93] https://www.jstor.org/stable/2151625
[94] https://www.jstor.org/stable/2701865
[95] https://www.jstor.org/stable/3054375
[96] https://www.whitehouse.gov/1600/presidents/dwightdeisenhower
[97] https://www.eisenhower.archives.gov/
[98] http://www.nps.gov/eise/index.htm
[99] https://vault.fbi.gov/dwight-david-ike-eisenhower
[100] http://eisenhowerfoundation.net/
[101] https://www.eisenhower.archives.gov/all_about_ike/speeches.html
[102] http://topics.nytimes.com/top/reference/timestopics/people/e/dwight_david_eisenhower/index.html
[103] https://www.loc.gov/rr/program/bib/presidents/eisenhower/index.html
[104] http://www.nato.int/cps/en/natohq/declassified_137961.htm
[105] http://millercenter.org/president/eisenhower
[106] http://www.c-span.org/video/?151630-1/life-portrait-dwight-d-eisenhower
[107] https://www.gutenberg.org/author/Eisenhower,+Dwight+D.+(Dwight+David)
[108] https://librivox.org/author/11301
[109] https//archive.org
[110] http://www.shapell.org/Collection/Presidents/Eisenhower-Dwight-D
[111] https://www.imdb.com/name/nm0252032/
[112] https://www.c-span.org/person/?dwighteisenhower
[113] http://purl.org/pressemappe20/folder/pe/004600
[114] //en.wikipedia.org/w/index.php?title=Template:Eisenhower_series&action=edit
[115] Pusey, p. 10.
[116] Pusey, pp. 7–8.
[117] Pach & Richardson, pp. 1–2.

[118] Ambrose, volume 1, p. 496.
[119] Pusey, pp. 11–12.
[120] Pach & Richardson, pp. 19–20.
[121] Pusey, p. 13.
[122] Pach & Richardson, pp. 20–21.
[123] Pusey, p. 23.
[124] Lyon, pp. 472–473.
[125] Pach & Richardson, p. 20.
[126] Pusey, p. 24.
[127] Lyon, p. 477.
[128] Pach & Richardson, pp. 22–23.
[129] Lyon, pp. 480–490.
[130] Morison, p. 1078.
[131] Pach & Richardson, pp. 26–27.
[132] Morison, pp. 1079–1083.
[133] Wicker, pp. 18–20.
[134] Pach & Richardson, pp. 39–40.
[135] Pach & Richardson, pp. 77–78.
[136] Pach & Richardson, p. 37.
[137] Pach & Richardson, pp. 35–36.
[138] Pach & Richardson, pp. 41–42.
[139] Wicker, pp. 47–48.
[140] Pach & Richardson, pp. 141–142.
[141] Richard Rhodes, "'Eisenhower' Review: An Artist in Iron," *Wall Street Journal* March 17, 2018 https://www.wsj.com/articles/eisenhower-review-an-artist-in-iron-1521144751 quoting William I. Hitchcock, "The Age of Eisenhower: America and the World in the 1950s" (2018).
[142] Herring 2008, pp. 651–652.
[143] Herring 2008, p. 665.
[144] Wicker, pp. 22–24, 44.
[145] Pach & Richardson, pp. 80–82.
[146] Patterson, pp. 208–210, 261.
[147] Patterson, pp. 210–215, 223–233.
[148] Patterson, pp. 232–233.
[149] Edward C. Keefer, "President Dwight D. Eisenhower and the End of the Korean War" *Diplomatic History* (1986) 10#3: 267–289; quote follows footnote 33.
[150] Herring 2008, pp. 660–661.
[151] Stephen M. Streeter, *Managing the Counterrevolution: The United States and Guatemala, 1954–1961* (Ohio UP, 2000), pp. 7–9, 20.
[152] Herring 2008, p. 657.
[153] Herring 2008, pp. 668–670.
[154] Herring 2008, pp. 664–668.
[155] Herring 2008, pp. 661–662.
[156] Patterson, pp. 292–293.
[157] Pach & Richardson, pp. 97–98.
[158] Patterson, pp. 296–298.
[159] Herring 2008, pp. 663–664, 693.
[160] Herring 2008, p. 692.
[161] Herring 2008, pp. 672–674.
[162] Pach & Richardson, pp. 126–128.
[163] Herring 2008, pp. 674–675.
[164] See Anthony Eden, and Dwight D. Eisenhower, *Eden-Eisenhower Correspondence, 1955–1957* (U of North Carolina Press, 2006)
[165] Pach & Richardson, pp. 129–130.
[166] Herring 2008, pp. 675–676.
[167] Pach & Richardson, p. 163.
[168] Patterson, p. 423.

[169] Herring 2008, pp. 678–679.
[170] Pach & Richardson, pp. 191–192.
[171] Herring 2008, pp. 679–681.
[172] Herring 2008, pp. 683–686.
[173] Herring 2008, pp. 686–67.
[174] Wicker, pp. 108–109.
[175] Herring 2008, pp. 688–689.
[176] Patterson, pp. 287–288.
[177] Peter J. Roman, *Eisenhower and the Missile Gap* (1996)
[178] Patterson, pp. 419–420.
[179] Keith W. Baum, "Two's Company, Three's a Crowd: The Eisenhower Administration, France, and Nuclear Weapons." *Presidential Studies Quarterly* 20#2 (1990): 315–328. in JSTOR https://www.jstor.org/stable/27550617
[180] Herring 2008, p. 670.
[181] Patterson, pp. 303–304.
[182] Herring 2008, pp. 696–698.
[183] Pach & Richardson, pp. 214–215.
[184] Bogle, Lori Lynn, ed. (2001), *The Cold War*, Routledge, p. 104. 978-0815337218
[185] International Boundary and Water Commission; Falcon Dam http://www.ibwc.state.gov/Organization/Operations/Field_Offices/Falcon.html
[186] Kabaservice, pp. 14–15.
[187] Pach & Richardson, pp. 50–51.
[188] Pach & Richardson, pp. 30–31.
[189] Pach & Richardson, pp. 53–55.
[190] Pach & Richardson, pp. 56–57.
[191] Pach & Richardson, p. 168.
[192] Smith, p. 648.
[193] Patterson, pp. 400–401.
[194] Kabaservice, pp. 17–18.
[195] All figures, except for debt percentage, are presented in billions of dollars. GDP is calculated for the calendar year. The income, outlay, deficit, and debt figures are calculated for the fiscal year, which ended on June 30 prior to 1976.
[196] Represents the national debt held by the public as a percentage of GDP
[197] Patterson, pp. 311–312.
[198] Patterson, p. 289.
[199] Patterson, p. 315.
[200] Patterson, pp. 326–327.
[201] Pach & Richardson, pp. 46–47.
[202] Pach & Richardson, pp. 17–18, 63.
[203] Pach & Richardson, pp. 62–63.
[204] Pach & Richardson, pp. 69–70.
[205] Pach & Richardson, pp. 70–71.
[206] Patterson, p. 270.
[207] Pach & Richardson, p. 64.
[208] Patterson, p. 264.
[209] Pach & Richardson, p. 65.
[210] Patterson, pp. 416–418.
[211] Patterson, pp. 380–383.
[212] Pach & Richardson, pp. 137–138.
[213] Herring 2008, pp. 681–682.
[214] Pach & Richardson, pp. 138–139.
[215] Smith, p. 710–711.
[216] Pach & Richardson, p. 140.
[217] Pach & Richardson, pp. 144–145.
[218] Patterson, pp. 389–394.
[219] Patterson, pp. 396–398.

[220] Pach & Richardson, pp. 145–146.
[221] Pach & Richardson, pp. 147–148.
[222] Patterson, p. 413.
[223] Pach & Richardson, pp. 148–150.
[224] Pach & Richardson, pp. 150–155.
[225] Pach & Richardson, pp. 156–157.
[226] Pach & Richardson, p. 157.
[227] http://www.fhwa.dot.gov/interstate/audiotext.htm#cadillac
[228] Patterson, p. 274.
[229] Smith, p. 652.
[230] Ambrose, volume 2, pp. 301, 326.
[231] Smith, pp. 652–653.
[232] Smith, pp. 651–654.
[233] Smith, p. 650.
[234] Schefter, pp. 3-5.
[235] Patterson, p. 418.
[236] Lyon, p. 805.
[237] Schefter, pp. 25–26.
[238] Patterson, pp. 325–326.
[239] Elizabeth A. Fones-Wolf, *Selling free enterprise: The business assault on labor and liberalism, 1945–60* (U of Illinois Press, 1994).
[240] Ronald L. Goldfarb, *Perfect Villains, Imperfect Heroes: Robert F. Kennedy's War Against Organized Crime* (2002).
[241] Alton R. Lee, *Eisenhower and Landrum-Griffin: A study in labor-management politics* (UP of Kentucky, 1990).
[242] Pach & Richardson, pp. 175–176.
[243] Pach & Richardson, pp. 180–182.
[244] Pach & Richardson, pp. 183–184.
[245] "D. C. Home Rule." http://library.cqpress.com/cqalmanac/cqal59-1335607 In CQ Almanac 1959, 15th ed., 09-312-09-313. Washington, DC: Congressional Quarterly, 1960. Retrieved May 31, 2017.
[246] Pach & Richardson, p. 58.
[247] Pach & Richardson, p. 180.
[248] Newton, *Eisenhower* pp. 196–99.
[249] Clarence G. Lasby, *Eisenhower's Heart Attack: How Ike Beat Heart Disease and Held on to the Presidency* (1997) pp. 57–113.
[250] Robert P. Hudson, "Eisenhower's Heart Attack: How Ike Beat Heart Disease and Held on to the Presidency (review)" *Bulletin of the History of Medicine* 72#1 (1998) pp. 161–162 online https://muse.jhu.edu/article/4010.
[251] R.H. Ferrell, *Ill-Advised: Presidential Health & Public Trust* (1992) pp. 53–150
[252] Pach & Richardson, pp. 113–114.
[253] Pach & Richardson, pp. 174–175.
[254] Newton, *Eisenhower* pp. 296, 309.
[255] Pach & Richardson, pp. 114–116.
[256] Pach & Richardson, pp. 119–121.
[257] Morison, p. 1088.
[258] Pach & Richardson, pp. 122–123.
[259] Pach & Richardson, pp. 124–125.
[260] Patterson, p. 305.
[261] Pach & Richardson, pp. 135–136.
[262] Patterson, p. 309.
[263] Pach & Richardson, p. 136.
[264] Pach & Richardson, pp. 226–227.
[265] John Kitch, "Eisenhower and Nixon: A Friendship of Unequals." *Perspectives on Political Science* 46#2 (2017): 101–107.
[266] Wicker, pp. 116–117.

[267] Patterson, pp. 434–439.
[268] John A. Farrell, *Richard Nixon: the life* (2017) pp to 89–90
[269] Pach & Richardson, pp. 228–229.
[270] Patterson, pp. 436–437.
[271] Pach & Richardson, pp. 229.
[272] Pach & Richardson, p. 230.
[273] Paul S. Holbo, and Robert W. Sellen, eds. *The Eisenhower era: the age of consensus* (1974), pp 1-2.
[274] John Lewis Gaddis, "He Made It Look Easy: 'Eisenhower in War and Peace', by Jean Edward Smith" https://www.nytimes.com/2012/04/22/books/review/eisenhower-in-war-and-peace-by-jean-edward-smith.html?_r=1&pagewanted=all, *New York Times Book Review*, April 20, 2012.
[275] //lccn.loc.gov/65-12468
[276] https://archive.org/stream/eisenhowerthepre002645mbp#page/n11/mode/2up
[277] //lccn.loc.gov/56-8365
[278] https://books.google.com/?id=Y7m6edRkG2EC&dq=isbn%3A0385492537
[279] https://www.amazon.com/Eisenhower-Peace-Jean-Edward-Smith/dp/140006693X/
[280] https://archive.org/details/eisenhowerwhiteh00newt
[281] https://www.amazon.com/Like-Ike-Presidential-Election-Elections/dp/0700624058/
[282] https://www.jstor.org/stable/27551734
[283] https://archive.org/details/eisenhowerera00holb
[284] https://www.amazon.com/Ike-McCarthy-Eisenhowers-Campaign-against/dp/1451686609/
[285] //www.worldcat.org/oclc/31206927
[286] //www.worldcat.org/oclc/43953970
[287] https://archive.org/details/wagingpeacehowei00robe
[288] https://www.questia.com/library/4902321/eisenhower-the-anti-communist-crusade
[289] //doi.org/10.1111/j.1741-5705.2004.00235.x
[290] //doi.org/10.1162/jcws.2008.10.4.37
[291] //doi.org/10.1080/14682745.2011.545603
[292] https://archive.org/details/reevaluatingeise00mela
[293] https://www.questia.com/library/7751318/cross-fire-the-eight-years-with-eisenhower
[294] https://www.questia.com/library/118938565/the-eden-eisenhower-correspondence-1955-1957
[295] https://eisenhower.press.jhu.edu/about/index.html
[296] https://archive.org/search.php?query=title%3A%28electronic%29%20AND%20creator%3A%28eisenhower%29
[297] http://cisupa.proquest.com/ws_display.asp?filter=upa_intermediate&item_id=%7B1D426C0A-1FEB-49EA-ADD8-84EED93255A0%7D
[298] http://eisenhower.archives.gov/Research/Finding_Aids/E.html

Article Sources and Contributors

The sources listed for each article provide more detailed licensing information including the copyright status, the copyright owner, and the license conditions.

Dwight D. Eisenhower *Source:* https://en.wikipedia.org/w/index.php?oldid=854119724 *License:* Creative Commons Attribution-Share Alike 3.0 *Contributors:* 49ersBelongInSanFrancisco, 564dude, AAABBB222, Acroterion, AdaCiccone, Adavidb, Ammyboi, Andymii, Another Believer, Anthony22, Anythingyouwant, Arjayay, Basteperk, Bellerophon5685, Bergeronp, Binksternet, Bndujwkwlw, Bokmanrocks01, Byteflush, C sterner, CLCStudent, CapnZapp, CaptainBillyCatPants, Caroca2, Chewings72, Chris the speller, Classicwiki, Claudevsq, ClueBot NG, Cmac0801, Cocohead781, Colonestarrice, Coltsfan, Corkythehornetfan, Curet115, Curly Turkey, DVdm, DarthZealous, Dave Dial, Dawnseeker2000, Donner60, Drdpw, Drewmutt, Emir of Wikipedia, Emiya1980, Ergo Sum, Favonian, Flix11, Frietjes, Gaarmyvet, GeeTeeBee, GoodDay, GreenC, Hanna Liu, Hessamnia, Hohum, Home Lander, Hoppyh, HotdogPi, Howard352, Howcheng, I dream of horses, Illegitimate Barrister, IronGargoyle, Jabberjaw, Jakehutton25, JamesBWatson3, JamesEG, Johnjoseph, Jon Kolbert, JonVidds, Jpgordon, Jprg1966, KNHaw, KaiserDog21, Kbabej, Keivan.f, Koncurrentkat, L293D, LegoFan506, Lieutcoluseng, Linkkerpar, LivinRealGüd, Lockesdonkey, LordVesuvius, MONGO, MZMcBride, Maczkopeti, Malayedit, Mandruss, Manushand, Master of Time, Mccapra, Mehendri Solon, MelanieN, Mild Bill Hiccup, Mooie24, Mr. Guye, Mrothman1998, Naraht, Neveselbert, Nihiltres, Nikkimaria, Onel5969, Onghai1929, OrangeBoy99, Orser67, Oshwah, Pastelitodepapa, Petrb, Pkhwcgs, Plateblock, PlyrStar93, Pricejb, Quakepotato, RA0808, RCTodd, RFD, RainFall, Raymond Leonard, RecapGrant, RevelationDirect, Riririan King of the Rails, Rjensen, Rodw, SNUGGUMS, Samuelcollthin, ScrapIronIV, SemiHypercube, Serols, Shellwood, SpanishSnake, Srich32977, Sruva123, Ssolbergj, Steve Lux, Jr., Steve03Mills, Stonewall.jonesy, Sunshineisles2, Swpb, The Oz Squire, The RedBurn, TheFreeWorld, Theinstantmatrix, Therequiembellishere, Throast, Tktru, ToBeFree, Tobby72, Toluwan, Truther1515, Tschild, TwoTwoHello, ViriiK, Volvlogia, Vsmith, Wa3pxx, Wikievil666, WrigglingWobat, ⌂, 133 anonymous edits 1

Presidency of Dwight D. Eisenhower *Source:* https://en.wikipedia.org/w/index.php?oldid=852250241 *License:* Creative Commons Attribution-Share Alike 3.0 *Contributors:* Adavidb, Atwarwiththem, BD2412, Bede735, Bender235, Billinghurst, Binksternet, Capt Jim, Cburnett, ClueBot NG, Coa coapuffs, Compfreak7, Crowish, Dcirovic, Dpm12, Drdpw, Ekriirkehere, Ergo Sum, Ericl, FDRMRZUSA, Funandtrvl, Funzork, GardenCosmos, Gilliam, Giraffedata, Gongshow, GorillaWarfare, GraemeLeggett, Graham11, Guest2625, HandsomeFella, Holdoffhunger, Infinite-patterns, InverseHypercube, Ira Leviton, Issyl0, JayJasper, Jim1138, JimMacAllistair, John of Reading, Kierzek, Lacon432, Look2See1, Mehendri Solon, Mitchurch, Mr.gangsta, MuhannadDarwish, Narky Blert, Neveselbert, NuclearWizard, Orser67, Peace In Mississippi, Phlar, Ptb1997, Purplebackpack89, Quintessential British Gentleman, Rjensen, Rjwilmsi, Roberticus, Rwendland, ShroudedSciuridae, Sport and politics, TJ Spyke, Tdadamemd, TheTimesAreAChanging, Tide rolls, Timmyshin, Tktru, TonyO13, Trorov, Tyrol5, Uglemat, Wbm1058, Wildcursive, Zictor23, 67 anonymous edits 69

Image Sources, Licenses and Contributors

The sources listed for each image provide more detailed licensing information including the copyright status, the copyright owner, and the license conditions.

Image *Source:* https://en.wikipedia.org/w/index.php?title=File:Dwight_D._Eisenhower,_official_photo_portrait,_May_29,_1959.jpg *License:* Public Domain *Contributors:* White House … 1

Image *Source:* https://en.wikipedia.org/w/index.php?title=File:Dwight_Eisenhower_Signature.svg *License:* Public Domain *Contributors:* Connormah, Dwight D. Eisenhower … 3

Image *Source:* https://en.wikipedia.org/w/index.php?title=File:Flag_of_the_United_States.svg *License:* Public Domain *Contributors:* Anomie, Jo-Jo Eumerus, MSGJ, Mr. Stradivarius … 3

Image *Source:* https://en.wikipedia.org/w/index.php?title=File:Flag_of_the_United_States_Army_(official_proportions).svg *License:* Public Domain *Contributors:* United States Army … 3

Image *Source:* https://en.wikipedia.org/w/index.php?title=File:US_Army_O11_shoulderboard_rotated.svg *License:* Public Domain *Contributors:* US_Army_O11_shoulderboard.svg: Ipankonin derivative work: Amirki (talk) … 3

Image *Source:* https://en.wikipedia.org/w/index.php?title=File:Distinguished_Service_Medal_ribbon.svg *Contributors:* - … 3

Image *Source:* https://en.wikipedia.org/w/index.php?title=File:Navy_Distinguished_Service_ribbon.svg *Contributors:* - … 3

Image *Source:* https://en.wikipedia.org/w/index.php?title=File:Legion_of_Merit_ribbon.svg *Contributors:* AlanM1, EclecticArkie, EricSerge, FSII, FieldMarine, Flamurai, Huntster, Illegitimate Barrister, Ipankonin, Sarang, Sportsfan92 … 3

Image *Source:* https://en.wikipedia.org/w/index.php?title=File:World_War_I_Victory_Medal_ribbon.svg *Contributors:* Ipankonin … 3

Image *Source:* https://en.wikipedia.org/w/index.php?title=File:World_War_II_Victory_Medal_ribbon.svg *Contributors:* Ipankonin … 3

Image *Source:* https://en.wikipedia.org/w/index.php?title=File:Seal_of_the_President_of_the_United_States.svg *License:* Public Domain *Contributors:* A.Savin, Aced, AnonMoos, Bjankuloski06en, BotMultichill, CastAStone, Clindberg, CouvGeek, Crasstun, DieBuche, Dschwen, Foroa, Fry1989, Gryffindor, Hautala, Illegitimate Barrister, Kwj2772, Mattflaschen, Multichill, NE2, Pmsyyz, Sarang, Simplyelegant events, Ssolbergj, TCY, WhisperToMe, Wsiegmund, 4 anonymous edits … 5

Image *Source:* https://en.wikipedia.org/w/index.php?title=File:US-O11_insignia.svg *License:* Public Domain *Contributors:* Ipankonin … 5

Image *Source:* https://en.wikipedia.org/w/index.php?title=File:Coat_of_Arms_of_Dwight_Eisenhower.svg *Contributors:* User:Glasshouse … 5

Figure 1 *Source:* https://en.wikipedia.org/w/index.php?title=File:Eisenhower_House.jpg *Contributors:* User:GorianEmpathy … 7

Figure 2 *Source:* https://en.wikipedia.org/w/index.php?title=File:Eisenhower_Football.jpg *License:* Public Domain *Contributors:* Docu, File Upload Bot (Magnus Manske), Hawkeye7, IngerAlHaosului, Morio, OgreBot 2, Richardkiwi, 2 anonymous edits … 9

Figure 3 *Source:* https://en.wikipedia.org/w/index.php?title=File:Mamie_eisenhower.gif *License:* Public Domain *Contributors:* Bastique, BotMultichill, CrazyPhunk, Evrik, Fred J, Happyme22, Jiang, MGA73, Pfctdayelise, Tktru, WFinch, 2 anonymous edits … 10

Figure 4 *Source:* https://en.wikipedia.org/w/index.php?title=File:Eisenhower_transcontinental_military_convoy.jpg *License:* Public Domain *Contributors:* Btphelps, Docu, Morio, 2 anonymous edits … 13

Figure 5 *Source:* https://en.wikipedia.org/w/index.php?title=File:Major_General_Dwight_Eisenhower,_1942_TR207.jpg *License:* Public Domain *Contributors:* Fæ, Labattblueboy, Rcbutcher, Teofilo, Thib Phil, 遼東半島 … 16

Figure 6 *Source:* https://en.wikipedia.org/w/index.php?title=File:Dwight_D._Eisenhower_as_General_of_the_Army_crop.jpg *License:* Public Domain *Contributors:* Signal Corps … 16

Figure 7 *Source:* https//en.wikipedia.org *License:* Public Domain *Contributors:* Mayyskiyysergeyy, Michael Barera, WFinch … 18

Figure 8 *Source:* https://en.wikipedia.org/w/index.php?title=File:Eisenhower_d-day.jpg *License:* Public Domain *Contributors:* Unknown U.S. Army photographer … 19

Figure 9 *Source:* https://en.wikipedia.org/w/index.php?title=File:American_World_War_II_senior_military_officials,_1945.JPEG *License:* Public Domain *Contributors:* Army; part of the collection of the Office of War Information … 20

Figure 10 *Source:* https://en.wikipedia.org/w/index.php?title=File:Allied_Commanders_after_Germany_Surrendered.jpg *License:* Public Domain *Contributors:* Not given (Army Signal Corps Collection) … 21

Figure 11 *Source:* https://en.wikipedia.org/w/index.php?title=File:American_Sector_Germany.png *License:* GNU Free Documentation License *Contributors:* User WikiNight from the German Wikipedia … 22

Figure 12 *Source:* https://en.wikipedia.org/w/index.php?title=File:General_Dwight_Eisenhower_in_Warsaw,_1945.jpg *License:* Public Domain *Contributors:* Central Photographic Agency (CAF) in Warsaw … 23

Figure 13 *Source:* https://en.wikipedia.org/w/index.php?title=File:Bundesarchiv_Bild_183-14059-0018,_Berlin,_Oberbefehlshaber_der_vier_Verbündeten.jpg *License:* Creative Commons Attribution-Share Alike 3.0 Germany *Contributors:* Alexrk2, BotMultichill, Butko, Catsmeat, Docu, Gkml, Jeff5102, Martin H., Mogelzahn, Morio, PDD, Palamède, Srittau, 4 anonymous edits … 25

Figure 14 *Source:* https://en.wikipedia.org/w/index.php?title=File:I_Like_Ike_button,_1952.png *License:* Creative Commons Attribution-Sharealike 3.0 *Contributors:* Tyrol5 … 27

Figure 15 *Source:* https://en.wikipedia.org/w/index.php?title=File:ElectoralCollege1952.svg *License:* Public Domain *Contributors:* BippyTheGuy, Citypeek, Oxam Hartog, RingtailedFox, SteveSims～commonswiki … 28

Figure 16 *Source:* https://en.wikipedia.org/w/index.php?title=File:Eisenhower_on_Hobo_Day.jpg *Contributors:* SDSU … 29

Figure 17 *Source:* https://en.wikipedia.org/w/index.php?title=File:ElectoralCollege1956.svg *License:* Public Domain *Contributors:* ChrisDHDR, Kmusser, Oxam Hartog, RingtailedFox, SteveSims～commonswiki … 30

Figure 18 *Source:* https://en.wikipedia.org/w/index.php?title=File:Dwight_D._Eisenhower,_White_House_photo_portrait,_February_1959.jpg *License:* Public Domain *Contributors:* Presumably a White House photographer, since it is in the Presidential years collection and no assertion of copyright is … 31

Image *Source:* https://en.wikipedia.org/w/index.php?title=File:Gnome-mime-sound-openclipart.svg *Contributors:* User:Eubulides … 33

Figure 19 *Source:* https://en.wikipedia.org/w/index.php?title=File:Indo_US.jpg *License:* Public Domain *Contributors:* AtelierMonpli, Badseed, Co9man, FSII, Fadesga, Frank C. Müller, Infrogmation, Mabdul, Perumalism, Rahulmit, Roland zh, Yann … 34

Figure 20 *Source:* https//en.wikipedia.org *Contributors:* Bgag, Billinghurst, Frank C. Müller, Gray eyes, J 1982, KOKUYO, Kai3952, Monopoly31121993, Morio, Skeezix1000, Solomon203, Vmenkov, Wangyunfeng, Wildcursive, Yerevanci, 玄史生 , 2 anonymous edits … 34

Figure 21 *Source:* https://en.wikipedia.org/w/index.php?title=File:President_Eisenhower_and_Nikita_Khrushchev_1959.jpg *License:* Public Domain *Contributors:* Associated Press … 35

Figure 22 *Source:* https://en.wikipedia.org/w/index.php?title=File:President_Dwight_D._Eisenhower,_Dr._von_Braun_and_Others.jpg *License:* Public Domain *Contributors:* Hohum, Morio, WvB77 … 37

Figure 23 *Source:* https://en.wikipedia.org/w/index.php?title=File:1951_Chung_Baik_Eisenhower.jpg *License:* Public Domain *Contributors:* Bigsidy, Dagollus, HappyMidnight, Hyolee2, Ideavnovich, Monopoly31121993, Zhuyifei1999 … 38

Figure 24 *Source:* https://en.wikipedia.org/w/index.php?title=File:ShahEisenhower.jpg *License:* Public Domain *Contributors:* Alborzagros, Chyah, Docu, Ervaude, Fadesga, Idranstel, Infrogmation, Man vyi, Monopoly31121993, Morio, SecretName101, Wvk, 2 anonymous edits … 40

Figure 25 *Source:* https://en.wikipedia.org/w/index.php?title=File:Eisenhower_and_Nixon_at_Dinner_with_King_Saud.jpg *License:* Public Domain *Contributors:* Hank Walker - The LIFE Picture Collection … 41

Figure 26 *Source:* https://en.wikipedia.org/w/index.php?title=File:US_Air_Force_U-2_(2139646280).jpg *License:* Public Domain *Contributors:* U.S. Air Force photo by Master Sgt. Rose Reynolds … 43

Figure 27 *Source:* https://en.wikipedia.org/w/index.php?title=File:Dwight_D._Eisenhower,_official_Presidential_portrait.jpg *License:* Public Domain *Contributors:* James Anthony Wills … 49

Figure 28 *Source:* https://en.wikipedia.org/w/index.php?title=File:Dwight_Eisenhower_at_1964_RNC_(cropped1).jpg *License:* Public Domain *Contributors:* Animalparty, OgreBot 2, SecretName101 … 51

Figure 29 *Source:* https://en.wikipedia.org/w/index.php?title=File:LBJ_and_Eisenhower.jpg *License:* Public Domain *Contributors:* Anthony22, Bossanoven, Botteville, Clusternote, DanTD, Governor Jerchel, Morio, SecretName101 … 52

Figure 30 *Source:* https://en.wikipedia.org/w/index.php?title=File:Funeral_services_for_Dwight_D._Eisenhower,_March_1969.jpg *License:* Public Domain *Contributors:* Atkins, Oliver F., 1916-1977, Photographer … 52

Figure 31 *Source:* https://en.wikipedia.org/w/index.php?title=File:DDEisenhowerGrave3.jpg *License:* Creative Commons Attribution-Sharealike 3.0 *Contributors:* User:CSvBibra … 53

Figure 32 *Source:* https://en.wikipedia.org/w/index.php?title=File:72-901-1_HR7786_Veterans_Day_June_1_1954.jpg *License:* Public Domain *Contributors:* U.S. Government … 55

Figure 33 *Source:* https//en.wikipedia.org *License:* Public Domain *Contributors:* Alonso de Mendoza, Globetrotter19, Illegitimate Barrister, Infrogmation, Morio … 56

Image *Source:* https://en.wikipedia.org/w/index.php?title=File:Dwight_D._Eisenhower_POTUS_Appreciation_Medal_Hawaii_Obverse.jpg *Contributors:* User:Waipahu96797 ... 57

Image *Source:* https://en.wikipedia.org/w/index.php?title=File:Dwight_D._Eisenhower_POTUS_Appreciation_Medal_Hawaii_Reverse.jpg *Contributors:* User:Waipahu96797 ... 57

Figure 34 *Source:* https://en.wikipedia.org/w/index.php?title=File:Eisenhower_Interstate_System_IMG_4192.JPG *License:* Creative Commons Attribution-Sharealike 3.0 *Contributors:* Billy Hathorn ... 58

Figure 35 *Source:* https://en.wikipedia.org/w/index.php?title=File:Eisenhower_bronze.jpg *License:* Public Domain *Contributors:* Jim Brothers 59

Figure 36 *Source:* https://en.wikipedia.org/w/index.php?title=File:Orden-Pobeda-Marshal_Vasilevsky.jpg *License:* Public Domain *Contributors:* Фред Искендеров ... 62

Figure 37 *Source:* https://en.wikipedia.org/w/index.php?title=File:Coat_of_Arms_of_Dwight_Eisenhower.svg *Contributors:* User:Glasshouse 62

Image *Source:* https://en.wikipedia.org/w/index.php?title=File:Mexican_Border_Service_Medal_ribbon.svg *Contributors:* Ipankonin ... 59

Image *Source:* https://en.wikipedia.org/w/index.php?title=File:American_Defense_Service_ribbon.svg *Contributors:* - ... 60

Image *Source:* https://en.wikipedia.org/w/index.php?title=File:Army_of_Occupation_ribbon.svg *Contributors:* Ipankonin ... 60

Image *Source:* https://en.wikipedia.org/w/index.php?title=File:ARG_Order_of_the_Liberator_San_Martin_-_Grand_Cross_BAR.png *License:* Public Domain *Contributors:* Wiki Romi ... 60

Image *Source:* https://en.wikipedia.org/w/index.php?title=File:AUT_Honour_for_Services_to_the_Republic_of_Austria_-_2nd_Class_BAR.png *License:* Public Domain *Contributors:* Wiki Romi ... 60

Image *Source:* https://en.wikipedia.org/w/index.php?title=File:Grand_Crest_Ordre_de_Leopold.png *License:* Public Domain *Contributors:* Wiki Romi ... 60

Image *Source:* https://en.wikipedia.org/w/index.php?title=File:Croix_de_Guerre_1940-1945_with_palm_(Belgium)_-_ribbon_bar.png *License:* Creative Commons Attribution 3.0 *Contributors:* McOleo ... 60

Image *Source:* https://en.wikipedia.org/w/index.php?title=File:BRA_Order_of_the_Southern_Cross_-_Grand_Cross_BAR.png *License:* Public Domain *Contributors:* Wiki Romi ... 60

Image *Source:* https://en.wikipedia.org/w/index.php?title=File:BRA_Ordem_do_Merito_Militar_Gra-cruz.png *Contributors:* User:EricSerge .. 60

Image *Source:* https://en.wikipedia.org/w/index.php?title=File:BRA_Ordem_do_Mérito_Aeronáutico_Grã-Cruz.png *Contributors:* User:EricSerge 60

Image *Source:* https://en.wikipedia.org/w/index.php?title=File:BRA_War_Medal.png *License:* Creative Commons Attribution-Sharealike 3.0 *Contributors:* User:EricSerge ... 60

Image *Source:* https://en.wikipedia.org/w/index.php?title=File:BRA_Campaign_Medal.png *License:* Creative Commons Attribution-Sharealike 3.0 *Contributors:* User:EricSerge ... 60

Image *Source:* https://en.wikipedia.org/w/index.php?title=File:CHL_Order_of_Merit_of_Chile_-_Grand_Cross_BAR.png *License:* Public Domain *Contributors:* AlanM1, Mimich, Sarang, Sportsfan92, Wiki Romi ... 60

Image *Source:* https://en.wikipedia.org/w/index.php?title=File:Order_of_the_Cloud_and_Banner_1st.gif *License:* Public domain *Contributors:* Sg647112c (talk) ... 60

Image *Source:* https://en.wikipedia.org/w/index.php?title=File:Czechoslovak_War_Cross_1939-1945_Ribbon.png *License:* Creative Commons Attribution-Sharealike 3.0 *Contributors:* Dandvsp (talk) ... 60

Image *Source:* https://en.wikipedia.org/w/index.php?title=File:Orderelefant_ribbon.png *License:* Public domain *Contributors:* Jakubkaja, Kei, Magog the Ogre, Portunes ... 60

Image *Source:* https://en.wikipedia.org/w/index.php?title=File:Order_of_Abdón_Calderón_1st_Class_(Ecuador)_-_ribbon_bar.png *License:* Creative Commons Attribution 3.0 *Contributors:* McOleo ... 60

Image *Source:* https://en.wikipedia.org/w/index.php?title=File:EGY_Order_of_Ismail.png *License:* Creative Commons Attribution-Sharealike 3.0 *Contributors:* User:EricSerge ... 60

Image *Source:* https://en.wikipedia.org/w/index.php?title=File:ETH_Order_of_Solomon_BAR.png *License:* Public Domain *Contributors:* Wiki Romi ... 60

Image *Source:* https://en.wikipedia.org/w/index.php?title=File:Order_of_The_Queen_of_Sheba_(Ethiopia)_ribbon.gif *License:* Creative Commons Attribution-Sharealike 3.0 *Contributors:* Ekapoj yam ... 60

Image *Source:* https://en.wikipedia.org/w/index.php?title=File:Legion_Honneur_GC_ribbon.svg *License:* Creative Commons Attribution-ShareAlike 3.0 Unported *Contributors:* Orem (wiki-pl: Orem, commons: Orem) ... 60

Image *Source:* https://en.wikipedia.org/w/index.php?title=File:Ruban_de_l'Ordre_de_la_Libération_(2).PNG *License:* GNU Free Documentation License *Contributors:* Paris75000 ... 60

Image *Source:* https://en.wikipedia.org/w/index.php?title=File:Medaille_militaire_ribbon.svg *License:* Creative Commons Attribution 3.0 *Contributors:* Boroduntalk ... 60

Image *Source:* https://en.wikipedia.org/w/index.php?title=File:Croix_de_guerre_1939–1945_stripe_bronsepalme.svg *License:* Creative Commons Attribution-Sharealike 3.0 *Contributors:* User:Ordensherre ... 60

Image *Source:* https://en.wikipedia.org/w/index.php?title=File:GRE_Order_of_George_I_-_Grand_Cross_BAR.png *License:* Creative Commons Zero *Contributors:* Wiki Romi ... 60

Image *Source:* https://en.wikipedia.org/w/index.php?title=File:GRE_Order_Redeemer_1Class.png *License:* Public Domain *Contributors:* Wiki Romi ... 60

Image *Source:* https://en.wikipedia.org/w/index.php?title=File:Guatemalan_Armed_Forces_Cross.jpg *License:* Creative Commons Attribution-Sharealike 3.0 *Contributors:* EHDI5YS (talk) ... 60

Image *Source:* https://en.wikipedia.org/w/index.php?title=File:Orden_Nacional_de_Honor_y_Mérito,_Gran_Cruz.svg *Contributors:* User:Trevor Goodchild ... 60

Image *Source:* https://en.wikipedia.org/w/index.php?title=File:OESSG_Cavaliere_di_Gran_Croce_BAR.jpg *License:* Creative Commons Attribution-Sharealike 3.0 *Contributors:* User:Delehaye ... 60

Image *Source:* https://en.wikipedia.org/w/index.php?title=File:Cavaliere_di_gran_Croce_BAR.svg *License:* Public Domain *Contributors:* F l a n k e r ... 61

Image *Source:* https://en.wikipedia.org/w/index.php?title=File:JPN_Daikun'i_kikkasho_BAR.svg *License:* Public Domain *Contributors:* Mimich 61

Image *Source:* https://en.wikipedia.org/w/index.php?title=File:Ordre_de_la_couronne_de_Chene_GC_ribbon.svg *License:* Creative Commons Attribution 3.0 *Contributors:* Boroduntalk ... 61

Image *Source:* https://en.wikipedia.org/w/index.php?title=File:LUX_Military_Medal_ribbon.PNG *License:* Creative Commons Attribution-Sharealike 3.0 *Contributors:* EricSerge ... 61

Image *Source:* https://en.wikipedia.org/w/index.php?title=File:OPMM-gcX.svg *License:* Creative Commons Attribution-Sharealike 3.0 *Contributors:* User:Arturolorioli ... 61

Image *Source:* https://en.wikipedia.org/w/index.php?title=File:MEX_Order_of_the_Aztec_Eagle_1Class_BAR.png *License:* Public Domain *Contributors:* Wiki Romi ... 61

Image *Source:* https://en.wikipedia.org/w/index.php?title=File:MEX_Condecoracion_al_Merito_Militar_Primera_Clase.png *Contributors:* User:EricSerge ... 61

Image *Source:* https://en.wikipedia.org/w/index.php?title=File:Noribbon.svg *License:* Creative Commons Attribution-Sharealike 3.0 *Contributors:* WillT.Net (talk) ... 61

Image *Source:* https://en.wikipedia.org/w/index.php?title=File:Ordre_de_l'Ouissam_Alaouite_GC_ribbon_(Maroc).svg *License:* Creative Commons Attribution 3.0 *Contributors:* Boroduntalk ... 61

Image *Source:* https://en.wikipedia.org/w/index.php?title=File:NLD_Order_of_the_Dutch_Lion_-_Grand_Cross_BAR.png *License:* Creative Commons Zero *Contributors:* Wiki Romi ... 61

Image *Source:* https://en.wikipedia.org/w/index.php?title=File:St_Olavs_Orden_storkors_stripe.svg *License:* Creative Commons Attribution-Sharealike 3.0 *Contributors:* Ordensherre ... 61

Image *Source:* https://en.wikipedia.org/w/index.php?title=File:Ord.Nishan-i-Pakistan.ribbon.gif *License:* Public Domain *Contributors:* LudovicusXIV ... 61

Image *Source:* https://en.wikipedia.org/w/index.php?title=File:PAN_Order_of_Manuel_Amador_Guerrero_-_Grand_Officer_BAR.png *License:* Public Domain *Contributors:* Wiki Romi ... 61

Image *Source:* https://en.wikipedia.org/w/index.php?title=File:PAN_Order_of_Vasco_Nunez_de_Balboa_-_Grand_Cross_BAR.png *License:* Public Domain *Contributors:* Wiki Romi ... 61

Image *Source:* https://en.wikipedia.org/w/index.php?title=File:PHL_Order_of_Sikatuna_-_Grand_Collar_BAR.png *License:* Public Domain *Contributors:* User:Wiki Romi ... 61

Image *Source:* https://en.wikipedia.org/w/index.php?title=File:PHL_Legion_of_Honor_-_Chief_Commander_BAR.png *License:* Public Domain *Contributors:* Wiki Romi ... 61

Image *Source:* https://en.wikipedia.org/w/index.php?title=File:PHL_Distinguished_Service_Star_BAR.png *License:* Public Domain *Contributors:* Wiki Romi ... 61

Image *Source:* https://en.wikipedia.org/w/index.php?title=File:POL_Polonia_Restituta_Wielki_BAR.svg *License:* Creative Commons Attribution-ShareAlike 3.0 Unported *Contributors:* User:Orem ... 61

Image *Source:* https://en.wikipedia.org/w/index.php?title=File:POL_Virtuti_Militari_Wielki_BAR.svg *License:* Creative Commons Attribution-ShareAlike 3.0 Unported *Contributors:* User:Orem ... 61

Image *Source:* https://en.wikipedia.org/w/index.php?title=File:POL_Order_Krzyża_Grunwaldu_1_Klasy_BAR.svg *License:* Creative Commons Attribution-ShareAlike 3.0 Unported *Contributors:* Author: Orem (wiki-pl: Orem, commons: Orem) ... 61

Image *Source:* https://en.wikipedia.org/w/index.php?title=File:Order_of_the_Royal_House_of_Chakri_(Thailand)_ribbon.png *License:* Public Domain *Contributors:* PalawanOz ... 61

Image *Source:* https://en.wikipedia.org/w/index.php?title=File:Ordre_du_Nichan_Iftikhar_GC_ribbon_(Tunisia).svg *License:* Creative Commons Attribution 3.0 *Contributors:* Boroduntalk ... 61

Image *Source:* https://en.wikipedia.org/w/index.php?title=File:Order_of_the_Bath_(ribbon).svg *Contributors:* - ... 61

Image *Source:* https://en.wikipedia.org/w/index.php?title=File:Order_of_Merit_(Commonwealth_realms)_ribbon.png *License:* Public Domain *Contributors:* en:User:Miesianiacal ... 61

Image *Source:* https://en.wikipedia.org/w/index.php?title=File:Africa_Star_8th_1st_BAR.svg *License:* Public Domain *Contributors:* Africa_Star_BAR.svg: Lubicz & Orem derivative work: Mboro (talk) ... 61

Image *Source:* https://en.wikipedia.org/w/index.php?title=File:Ordervictory_rib.png *License:* Public Domain *Contributors:* Dpkg95, EugeneZelenko, Ilich, Mariluna, Sportsfan92, Wiki Romi, Zscout370, Георгий Долгопский ... 61

Image *Source:* https://en.wikipedia.org/w/index.php?title=File:Order_of_Suvorov_106x30.png *License:* Creative Commons Attribution-Sharealike 3.0 *Contributors:* User:EricSerge ... 61

Image *Source:* https://en.wikipedia.org/w/index.php?title=File:The_Royal_Yugoslav_Commemorative_War_Cross_rib.png *License:* Public Domain *Contributors:* Snake bgd ... 61

Image *Source:* https://en.wikipedia.org/w/index.php?title=File:US-O2_insignia.svg *License:* Public Domain *Contributors:* Yaddah (talk) ... 63

Image *Source:* https://en.wikipedia.org/w/index.php?title=File:US-O3_insignia.svg *License:* Public Domain *Contributors:* Ipankonin ... 63

Image *Source:* https://en.wikipedia.org/w/index.php?title=File:US-O4_insignia.svg *License:* Public Domain *Contributors:* Ipankonin ... 63

Image *Source:* https://en.wikipedia.org/w/index.php?title=File:US-O5_insignia.svg *License:* Public Domain *Contributors:* Ipankonin ... 63

Image *Source:* https://en.wikipedia.org/w/index.php?title=File:US-O6_insignia.svg *License:* Public Domain *Contributors:* U.S. Defense Logistics Agency ... 64

Image *Source:* https://en.wikipedia.org/w/index.php?title=File:US-O7_insignia.svg *License:* Public Domain *Contributors:* Ipankonin ... 64

Image *Source:* https://en.wikipedia.org/w/index.php?title=File:US-O8_insignia.svg *License:* Public Domain *Contributors:* Ipankonin ... 64

Image *Source:* https://en.wikipedia.org/w/index.php?title=File:US-O9_insignia.svg *License:* Public Domain *Contributors:* Ipankonin ... 64

Image *Source:* https://en.wikipedia.org/w/index.php?title=File:US-O10_insignia.svg *License:* Public Domain *Contributors:* Ipankonin ... 64

Image *Source:* https://en.wikipedia.org/w/index.php?title=File:Speaker_Icon.svg *License:* Public Domain *Contributors:* User:Mobius ... 68

Image *Source:* https://en.wikipedia.org/w/index.php?title=File:Blue_pencil.svg *License:* Public Domain *Contributors:* User:VasilievVV and user:Jarekt ... 68

Figure 38 *Source:* https://en.wikipedia.org/w/index.php?title=File:I_like_Ike.jpg *License:* Public Domain *Contributors:* Credit: Dwight D. Eisenhower Library ... 73

Figure 39 *Source:* https://en.wikipedia.org/w/index.php?title=File:ElectoralCollege1952.svg *License:* Public Domain *Contributors:* BippyTheGuy, Citypeek, Oxam Hartog, RingtailedFox, SteveSims～commonswiki ... 76

Figure 40 *Source:* https://en.wikipedia.org/w/index.php?title=File:Earl_Warren.jpg *License:* Public Domain *Contributors:* Harris & Ewing photography firm ... 80

Figure 41 *Source:* https://en.wikipedia.org/w/index.php?title=File:Cold_War_WorldMap_1953.png *License:* GNU Free Documentation License *Contributors:* BD2412, OgreBot 2 ... 82

Figure 42 *Source:* https://en.wikipedia.org/w/index.php?title=File:Eisenhower_inspects_YB52.jpg *License:* Public Domain *Contributors:* USAF 83

Figure 43 *Source:* https//en.wikipedia.org *Contributors:* Bgag, Billinghurst, Frank C. Müller, Gray eyes, J 1982, KOKUYO, Kai3952, Monopoly31121993, Morio, Skeezix1000, Solomon203, Vmenkov, Wangyunfeng, Wildcursive, Yerevanci, 玄史生 , 2 anonymous edits ... 87

Figure 44 *Source:* https://en.wikipedia.org/w/index.php?title=File:Thor_first_launch.jpg *License:* Public Domain *Contributors:* USAF ... 91

Figure 45 *Source:* https://en.wikipedia.org/w/index.php?title=File:US_President_Dwight_Eisenhower_Presidential_Trips.PNG *License:* Public domain *Contributors:* Spry895 (talk) ... 93

Image *Source:* https://en.wikipedia.org/w/index.php?title=File:Flag_of_South_Korea_(1949–1984).png *License:* Public Domain *Contributors:* HeneralVicente23, Illegitimate Barrister, Jo-Jo Eumerus, RainbowSilver2ndBackup, 1 anonymous edits ... 94

Image *Source:* https://en.wikipedia.org/w/index.php?title=File:Flag_of_Mexico_(1934–1968).png *License:* Public Domain *Contributors:* AtomicIce, Fry1989, Illegitimate Barrister, Kimdime, とある白い猫 , 1 anonymous edits ... 94

Image *Source:* https://en.wikipedia.org/w/index.php?title=File:Canadian_Red_Ensign_(1921–1957).svg *License:* Public Domain *Contributors:* User:Denelson83 ... 94

Image *Source:* https://en.wikipedia.org/w/index.php?title=File:Flag_of_Bermuda_1910.svg *Contributors:* - ... 94

Image *Source:* https://en.wikipedia.org/w/index.php?title=File:Flag_of_Switzerland.svg *License:* Public Domain *Contributors:* User:Marc Mongenet Credits: User:-xfi- User:Zscout370 ... 94

Image *Source:* https://en.wikipedia.org/w/index.php?title=File:Flag_of_Panama.svg *License:* Public Domain *Contributors:* -xfi-, Addicted04, Alkari, Bast64～commonswiki, Benzoyl, Blackcat, Cathy Richards, CemDemirkartal, Comandante777, Cycn, Duduziq, Fadi the philologer, FreshCorp619, Fry1989, Geagea, Golden Bosnian Lily, Huhsunqu, Hystrix, Joshbaumgartner, Klemen Kocjancic, Liftarn, Mattes, NicoScribe, Nightstallion, Ninane, Pumbaa80, Reisio, Rfc1394, Sangjinhwa, SiBr4, TFCforever, TFerenczy, Taichi, Thomas81, ThomasPusch, Zscout370, Ö, Фёдор Гусляров, 27 anonymous edits ... 94

Image *Source:* https://en.wikipedia.org/w/index.php?title=File:Flag_of_France.svg *License:* Public Domain *Contributors:* Anomie, Fastily, Jo-Jo Eumerus ... 94

Image *Source:* https://en.wikipedia.org/w/index.php?title=File:Flag_of_Germany.svg *License:* Public Domain *Contributors:* Anomie, Jo-Jo Eumerus 94

Image *Source:* https://en.wikipedia.org/w/index.php?title=File:Flag_of_the_United_Kingdom.svg *License:* Public Domain *Contributors:* Anomie, Good Olfactory, Jo-Jo Eumerus, MSGJ, Mifter ... 94

Image *Source:* https://en.wikipedia.org/w/index.php?title=File:Flag_of_Italy.svg *License:* Public Domain *Contributors:* Anomie, Jo-Jo Eumerus 94

Image *Source:* https://en.wikipedia.org/w/index.php?title=File:Flag_of_the_Vatican_City.svg *License:* Public Domain *Contributors:* AguaitantPV～commonswiki, Cathy Richards, Consta, Cycn, DenghiùComm, Denniss, Durin, F l a n k e r, Fry1989, Fulvio314, GoldenRainbow, HoheHoffnungen, Homo lupus, InfattiVedeteCheViDice, Jarekt, Jed, Klemen Kocjancic, Krun, Liftarn, Ludger1961, Mattes, Next2u, NielsF, Nightstallion, OAlexander～commonswiki, P-JR, Pumbaa80, RainbowSilver2ndBackup, Ravenpuff, Ricordisamoa, Robin van der Vliet, SiBr4, Steinsplitter, Str4nd, TFerenczy, Tacsipacsi, WikiDan61, Zscout370, Эрманарих, علی المزارقه, 22 anonymous edits ... 95

Image *Source:* https://en.wikipedia.org/w/index.php?title=File:Flag_of_Turkey.svg *License:* Public Domain *Contributors:* User:Dbenbenn ... 95

Image *Source:* https://en.wikipedia.org/w/index.php?title=File:Flag_of_Pakistan.svg *License:* Public Domain *Contributors:* User:Zscout370 ... 95

Image *Source:* https://en.wikipedia.org/w/index.php?title=File:Flag_of_Afghanistan_(1931–1973).svg *License:* Public Domain *Contributors:* at en.wikipedia. ... 95

Image *Source:* https://en.wikipedia.org/w/index.php?title=File:Flag_of_India.svg *License:* Public Domain *Contributors:* Anomie, Jo-Jo Eumerus, Mifter ... 95

Image *Source:* https://en.wikipedia.org/w/index.php?title=File:State_Flag_of_Iran_(1925).svg *Contributors:* - ... 95

Image *Source:* https://en.wikipedia.org/w/index.php?title=File:Flag_of_Greece_(1822-1978).svg *License:* Public Domain *Contributors:* (of code) User:Makaristos ... 95

Image *Source:* https://en.wikipedia.org/w/index.php?title=File:Flag_of_Tunisia_(1959–1999).svg *License:* Public domain *Contributors:* Orange Tuesday at en.wikipedia ... 95

Image *Source:* https://en.wikipedia.org/w/index.php?title=File:Flag_of_Spain_(1945–1977).svg *License:* Creative Commons Attribution-Share Alike *Contributors:* User:SanchoPanzaXXI ... 95

Image *Source:* https://en.wikipedia.org/w/index.php?title=File:Flag_of_Morocco.svg *License:* Public Domain *Contributors:* Anime Addict AA, AymanFlad, Barryob, Bgag, Cimoi, Cycn, Denelson83, Denniss, Djampa, Doodledoo, Earth Resident, EugeneZelenko, Fastily, Flad, Foroa, Fred J, Fry1989, Gmaxwell, Herbythyme, Klemen Kocjancic, Krinkle, Leyo, Mattes, Meno25, Mindspillage, Myself488, Odder, Offnfopt, Omar-toons, Orrling, OsamaK, Permjak, Ppntori, Reisio, Rodejong, Sangjinhwa, Sarang, SiBr4, Steinsplitter, Str4nd, TFCforever, ThomasPusch, Vispec, Xiquet, Yougarten, Zscout370, ～riley, 11 anonymous edits ... 95

Image *Source:* https://en.wikipedia.org/w/index.php?title=File:Flag_of_Brazil_(1889–1960).svg *License:* Public Domain *Contributors:* Artix Kreiger 2, Cycn, FSII, FreshCorp619, Fry1989, Guilherme Paula, Homo lupus, Illegitimate Barrister, Marcos Elias de Oliveira Júnior, Pixeltoo, Sangjinhwa, Shadowxfox, The ed17, TigerTjäder, Xufanc ... 95

Image *Source:* https://en.wikipedia.org/w/index.php?title=File:Flag_of_Argentina.svg *Contributors:* ALE!, Alkari, Allforrous, Barcex, Bencmq, Bobika, Cambalachero, Cathy Richards, Courcelles, Dbenbenn, Denelson83, Eugenio Hansen, OFS, Fanghong, Fma12, FreshCorp619, Fry1989, Geger54, Golden Bosnian Lily, GoldenRainbow, Hambrientino, HoheHoffnungen, Huhsunqu, INeverCry, Jarould, Jdx, Klemen Kocjancic, Kved, Kwpolska,

Lankiveil, LechitaPL, MAXXX-309, Maks Stirlitz, Nagy, Neq00, Nickitoolivares, Niridya, Odder, Philosophenschule des Platon, Prev, Pumbaa80, Reisio, Richardkiwi, Sarang, SiBr4, Smaug the Golden, Steinsplitter, TFerenczy, TigerTjäder, Yaddah, ZooFari, Zscout370, 26 anonymous edits 95
Image *Source:* https://en.wikipedia.org/w/index.php?title=File:Flag_of_Chile.svg *License:* Public Domain *Contributors:* Alkari, Andres gb.ldc, B1mbo, Benzoyl, BotMultichill, Cathy Richards, Cycn, David Newton, Dbenbenn, Denelson83, Er Komandante, Fibonacci, File Upload Bot (Magnus Manske), FreshCorp619, Fry1989, GoldenRainbow, Herbythyme, Huhsunqu, Kallerna, Kanonkas, Klemen Kocjancic, Kwasura, Kyro, LechitaPL, Leyo, MAXXX-309, Mattes, McZusatz, Mozzan, Nagy, Nightstallion, Perhelion, Piastu, Pixeltoo, Pumbaa80, SKopp, Sangjinhwa, Sarang, SiBr4, Smaug the Golden, Srtxg, Sterling.M.Archer, Str4nd, Tcfc2349, Ultratomio, VulpesVulpes42, Vzb83∼commonswiki, Xarucoponce, Yakoo, Yonatanh, Zscout370, 55 anonymous edits 95
Image *Source:* https://en.wikipedia.org/w/index.php?title=File:Flag_of_Uruguay.svg *License:* Public Domain *Contributors:* User:Reisio (original author) 95
Image *Source:* https://en.wikipedia.org/w/index.php?title=File:Flag_of_Portugal.svg *License:* Public Domain *Contributors:* Columbano Bordalo Pinheiro (1910; generic design); Vítor Luís Rodrigues; António Martins-Tuválkin (2004; this specific v 95
Image *Source:* https://en.wikipedia.org/w/index.php?title=File:Flag_of_the_Philippines_(navy_blue).svg *License:* Creative Commons Attribution-Sharealike 2.5 *Contributors:* Alkari, Billinghurst, FakirNL, FreshCorp619, Jeenim, Kurrop, Ljmajer, Lokal Profil, MGA73bot2, Mattes, Patstuart, SiBr4, Tcfc2349, User 50, 2 anonymous edits 95
Image *Source:* https://en.wikipedia.org/w/index.php?title=File:Flag_of_the_Republic_of_China.svg *License:* Public Domain *Contributors:* User:SKopp 96
Image *Source:* https://en.wikipedia.org/w/index.php?title=File:Flag_of_South_Korea.svg *License:* Public Domain *Contributors:* Various 96
Figure 46 *Source:* https://en.wikipedia.org/w/index.php?title=File:Eisenhower_in_the_Oval_Office.jpg *License:* Public Domain *Contributors:* Elton Lord 97
Figure 47 *Source:* https://en.wikipedia.org/w/index.php?title=File:101st_Airborne_at_Little_Rock_Central_High.jpg *License:* Public Domain *Contributors:* US Army 102
Figure 48 *Source:* https://en.wikipedia.org/w/index.php?title=File:Highways1955.gif *License:* Public Domain *Contributors:* FlickreviewR, Intelati, Ljthefro, Lymantria 104
Figure 49 *Source:* https://en.wikipedia.org/w/index.php?title=File:United_States_1959-08-present.png *License:* Creative Commons Attribution-ShareAlike 3.0 Unported *Contributors:* Made by User:Golbez. 108
Figure 50 *Source:* https://en.wikipedia.org/w/index.php?title=File:Gallup_Poll-Approval_Rating-Dwight_D_Eisenhower.png *License:* Public domain *Contributors:* BD2412, OgreBot 2, SecretName101, Zaccarias 109
Figure 51 *Source:* https://en.wikipedia.org/w/index.php?title=File:ElectoralCollege1956.svg *License:* Public Domain *Contributors:* ChrisDHDR, Kmusser, Oxam Hartog, RingtailedFox, SteveSims∼commonswiki 110
Figure 52 *Source:* https://en.wikipedia.org/w/index.php?title=File:ElectoralCollege1960.svg *License:* Public Domain *Contributors:* BippyTheGuy, ChrisDHDR, Kmusser, Oxam Hartog, RingtailedFox, SteveSims∼commonswiki, Will Be Continued 111

License

Creative Commons Attribution-Share Alike 3.0
//creativecommons.org/licenses/by-sa/3.0/

Index

ABC Records, 59
Abd al-Karim Qasim, 90
Abdul Qadeer Khan, 92
Abilene High School (Abilene, Kansas), 8
Abilene, Kansas, 2, 7, 8, 53
Abraham Lincoln, 11
Acapulco, 94
Act of Congress, 56
Adlai Stevenson II, 5, 29, 71, 74
Admiral of the fleet (Royal Navy), 57
Admiralty Tunnel, 15
Adolfo López Mateos, 94
Adolfo Ruiz Cortines, 94
Afghanistan, 95
AFL–CIO, 106
Africa Star, 61
Agra, 95
Agricultural Act of 1954, 96
Air Force One, 32, 52
Aksel Nielsen, 80
Alaska, 47, 107
Alaska Statehood Act, 107
Albert Nofi, 120
Alfred Gruenther, 11
Allen Dulles, 120
Allied advance from Paris to the Rhine, 5
Allied Control Council, 25
Allied Force Headquarters, 15
Allied invasion of Sicily, 17
Allied-occupied Austria, 86
Allied-occupied Germany, 22
Allies of World War II, 17
Alps, 19
American Battle Monuments Commission, 14
American Civil War, 12
American Defense Service Medal, 60
American Federation of Labor, 106
American occupation zone, 22
American Political Science Association, 113
American Presidents: Life Portraits, 68
Américo Tomás, 95
Aneurysm, 48
Angels in the Outfield (1951 film), 11
Anglicized, 6

Ankara, 95
Anthony Eden, 86, 94
Antonio Segni, 94
Aphasia, 48
Apostolic Palace, 95
Arab nationalism, 89, 90
Arab World, 88
Argentina, 95
Arizona, 99
Arkansas, 45
Arkansas Army National Guard, 45
Armed Forces of the United States, 44, 100
Armistice, 5
Armistice Day, 55
Armistice (July 1953 – November 1954), 4, 70
Armistice of 11 November 1918, 12
Army Distinguished Service Medal, 59
Army–McCarthy hearings, 100
Army of Occupation Medal, 60
Army of the United States, 64
Arthur E. Summerfield, 77, 78
Arthur S. Flemming, 77
Arthur Tedder, 1st Baron Tedder, 2
Arturo Frondizi, 95
Astronaut, 106
Aswan Dam, 89
Athens, 95
Atomic bomb, 23
Atoms for Peace, 4, 35, 70, 83
Attack on Pearl Harbor, 15
Augusta National Golf Club, 10, 26
Austria, 86
Austrian State Treaty, 86
Autobahn, 58
Awards and decorations, 3
Axis powers, 17
Ayub Khan (Field Marshal), 95

B-52 Stratofortress, 83
Bachelor of Science, 3
Baghdad Pact, 88
Baik Seon-yup, 38
Balmoral Castle, 94
Barry Goldwater, 53, 86

Battalion, 13
Battle of Berlin, 22
Battle of Dien Bien Phu, 87
Battle of Kasserine Pass, 17
Battle of the Bulge, 21
Battle of the Scheldt, 21
Bay of Pigs Invasion, 6, 36, 56
Benito Mussolini, 17
Benito Nardone, 95
Berlin, 92
Bermuda, 94
Bermuda Conference, 94
Bernard Baruch, 105
Bernard Montgomery, 17, 21, 25
Bernard Montgomery, 1st Viscount Montgomery of Alamein, 12, 14
Blanche Wiesen Cook, 25
Board of education, 102
Bolesław Bierut, 24
Bond (finance), 103
Bonn, 94
Bonus March, 14
Boone, Iowa, 10
Brasília, 95
Brazil, 95
Bricker Amendment, 46, 85
Brigadier general (United States), 15, 64
British Raj, 90
Brown v. Board of Education, 45, 81, 101
Buddha Records, 59
Buenos Aires, 95

Caedmon Audio, 59
Caisson (military), 53
California, 99
Camille Chamoun, 41
Campaign star, 60
Camp Colt, Pennsylvania, 12
Camp David, 10, 11, 56
Camp Meade, 12
Canada, 94
Cape Canaveral Air Force Station Space Launch Complex 17, 91
Capitol Rotunda, 53
Captain (United States O-3), 63
Captain (U.S. Army), 12
Carlisle Indians football, 9
Carlo DEste, 64
Carlos P. Garcia, 95
Carl von Clausewitz, 13
Casablanca, 95
CBS, 80
Celâl Bayar, 95
Central High School (Little Rock), 102
Central Intelligence Agency, 72, 85
Chairman of the Joint Chiefs of Staff, 26

Chance for Peace speech, 33, 82
Charles de Gaulle, 21, 44, 92, 94
Charles Douglas Jackson, 86
Charles Erwin Wilson, 77, 78
Charles Evans Whittaker, 47, 81
Checkers speech, 29, 75
Chequers, 94
Chiang Kai-shek, 34, 87
Chicago, 58, 74, 110
Chief Justice of the United States, 80, 81
Chief of staff (military), 14
Chief of Staff of the United States Army, 2, 5
Chile, 60, 95
Cholecystitis, 49
Christian Herter, 76
Chung Il-kwon, 38
Chushi Gangdruk, 88
CITEREFAmbrose, volume 1, 122
CITEREFAmbrose, volume 2, 124
CITEREFHerring2008, 122, 123
CITEREFKabaservice, 123
CITEREFLyon, 122, 124
CITEREFMorison, 122, 124
CITEREFPachRichardson, 121–125
CITEREFPatterson, 122–125
CITEREFPusey, 121, 122
CITEREFSchefter, 124
CITEREFSmith, 123, 124
CITEREFWicker, 122–124
Ciudad Acuña, 96
Civil rights, 54
Civil Rights Act of 1875, 45
Civil Rights Act of 1957, 4, 6, 45, 71, 101
Civil Rights Act of 1960, 45, 103
Civil Rights Commission, 45
Civitan International, 63
Clifford Roberts, 11
Coat of arms, 62
Coattail effect, 111
Coca-Cola Corporation, 26
COINTELPRO, 100
Cold turkey, 48
Cold War, 33, 35, 41, 73
Cold War (1953–62), 4, 70
Cold War strategy, 72, 83
Colonel (United States), 64
Columbia University, 5, 24
Command and General Staff College, 13
Commandant of the Coast Guard, 121
Commandant of the Marine Corps, 121
Commanding officer, 14
Communism, 37
Communist Party of Cuba, 91
Congestive heart failure, 53
Congo Crisis, 36
Congress of Industrial Organizations, 106

Conservatism in the United States, 6, 72
Conservative Coalition, 106
Containment, 85
Continental Oil, 26
Continuity of government, 79
Contract bridge, 11
Controlled-access highway, 33
Conventional weapon, 72, 83
Coombe, Kingston upon Thames, 15, 119
Council on Foreign Relations, 25
Court-martial, 13
Covert operation, 85
Credit card, 98
Crohns disease, 48
Croix de guerre 1939–1945, 60
Cross of Grunwald, 61
Cross of Military Merit, 60
Crusade in Europe, 3, 24, 67, 70
C-SPAN, 68, 113
Cuba, 91
Cuban Revolution, 91
Culzean Castle, 61, 94
Czechoslovakia, 22, 60
Czechoslovak War Cross 1939–1945, 60

DARPA, 4, 71
David Eisenhower, 10
David Owen (author), 119
Declaration of Neutrality, 86
Decolonization, 100
Decoration of Honour for Services to the Republic of Austria, 60
Defense Advanced Research Projects Agency, 105
Deficit spending, 6
Democratic Party (United States), 27, 71
Denison, Texas, 2, 5, 7
Denver, 58
Denver, Colorado, 10
Department of Defense (United States), 105
Desegregation, 44, 72, 100
Détente, 92
Deterrence theory, 72, 73, 83
Dien Bien Phu, 42
Digital object identifier, 116
Diplomatic missions of Belgium, 10
Disarmed Enemy Forces, 23
Disenfranchisement after the Reconstruction Era, 101
Distinguished Service Medal (United States Navy), 3
Distinguished Service Medal (U.S. Army), 3, 12
Distinguished Service Star, 61
District of Columbia, 45
Domino theory, 4, 36, 70, 87

Donald Trump, 29
Doubleday (publisher), 114
Doud Eisenhower, 2, 10
Douglas MacArthur, 13, 14, 56
Douglas McKay, 77, 78
Dow Jones Industrial Average, 98
Draft Eisenhower, 28
Draft Eisenhower movement, 4, 70, 73
Dual carriageway, 103
Dwight David Eisenhower and American Power, 66, 115
Dwight D. Eisenhower, **1**, 3, 69–72
Dwight D. Eisenhower (Brothers), 59
Dwight D. Eisenhower Memorial, 59
Dwight D. Eisenhower Presidential Library, Museum and Boyhood Home, 2, 4, 71
Dwight D. Eisenhower School for National Security and Resource Strategy, 14, 58

Earl Warren, 47, 72, 80
Early life and education, 3, 70
Eastern Bloc, 82, 83
Eastern United States, 73
Ecuador, 60
Edgar Faure, 94
Edgar N. Eisenhower, 8
Edward Hazlett, 8
E. Frederic Morrow, 101
Egyptian revolution of 1952, 89
Eighth Army (United Kingdom), 17
Eisenhower commemorative dollar, 58
Eisenhower Decides To Run, 66, 115
Eisenhower Doctrine, 4, 40, 71, 89
Eisenhower dollar, 58
Eisenhower jacket, 54
Eisenhower Presidential Library, 53
Eisenhowers farewell address, 4, 6, 50, 71, 112
Eisenhower Tunnel, 58
Electoral College (United States), 107
Elizabeth II, 94
Ely Culbertson, 11
Emerging technologies, 105
Empire of Japan, 15
End of World War II in Europe, 19, 33
English, 5
Episcopal Church in the United States of America, 53
Ernest J. King, 18
Erwin Rommel, 17
Estes Kefauver, 110
Ethiopian Empire, 60
Eurasia, 73
European-African-Middle Eastern Campaign Medal, 60
European Defence Community, 36, 86
European Theater of Operations, 15

135

Executive officer, 15
Executive Order 10450, 45
Executive privilege, 6, 46
Expenditures in the United States federal budget, 98
Explorer 1, 105
Explorers program, 105
Ezra Taft Benson, 77, 78, 80

Fair Deal, 96
Faisal I of Iraq, 90
Falcon Dam, 94
Federal-Aid Highway Act of 1944, 33
Federal Aid Highway Act of 1956, 33, 103
Federal Bureau of Investigation, 100
Federal Reserve Board of Governors, 80, 98
Federal Trade Commission, 107
Felix Frankfurter, 81
Fernand Bonnier de La Chapelle, 17
Fidel Castro, 36, 91
Field Marshal, 21
Field marshal (United Kingdom), 57
File:Cadillacsquareexcerpt.ogg, 33, 103
File:Dwight D. Eisenhowers first Inaugural Address, 1953-01-20.ogg, 3
First inauguration of Dwight D. Eisenhower, 3, 4, 70
First inauguration of Richard Nixon, 53
First Indochina War, 6, 42, 87
First National City Bank, 80
First Taiwan Strait Crisis, 88
Fiscal conservatism, 98
Five-star rank, 56
Former Presidents Act, 49
Formosa Resolution of 1955, 6
Fort Benning, 13
Fort Leavenworth, 13
Fort Lesley J. McNair, 58
Fort Lewis, 14, 15
Fort Sam Houston, 12
Fox Conner, 13
France, 94, 95
France and weapons of mass destruction, 92
Frances Perkins, 78
Francisco Franco, 87, 95
Francis Gary Powers, 43, 93
François Darlan, 17
Frank D. Fackenthal, 2
Frankfurt am Main, 22
Frank Gasparro, 57
Frank Gehry, 59
Franklin D. Roosevelt, 17, 18, 33
Frank Pace, 80
Frank Stanton (executive), 80
Fraternization, 23
Fred A. Seaton, 77

Frederick H. Mueller, 77
Fred M. Vinson, 81
Freedom of the City of London, 63
French Armed Forces, 17
French Indochina, 42
Fulgencio Batista, 91
Funeral train, 53

Gallup (company), 107, 109
Gallup poll, 109
Gallups List of Widely Admired People, 63
Gamal Abdel Nasser, 40, 89
Gasoline, 103
G. David Schine, 100
General Dynamics, 80
Generalfeldmarschall, 17
General Foods, 26
General Motors, 78
General officer, 9
General of the Army (United States), 3, 5, 21, 51, 58, 64
General (United Kingdom), 17
General (United States), 64
Geneva, 94
Geneva Conference (1954), 88
Geneva Summit (1955), 92, 94
George Marshall, 2, 13, 14, 54, 56
George Meany, 106
George M. Humphrey, 30, 77, 78
George P. Baker, 80
George S. Patton, 2, 13, 14, 18, 19
George S. Patton slapping incidents, 19
George Washington, 11, 120
Georgia (U.S. state), 12, 13
Georgy Malenkov, 82
Georgy Zhukov, 21, 25
Gerald Ford, 56
German Instrument of Surrender, 3, 21, 70
German National Library of Economics, 68
Gettysburg, Pennsylvania, 12, 51
Giovanni Gronchi, 94
Grayson L. Kirk, 2
Great Depression, 14
Greece, 95
Greek Civil War, 24
Grinnell College, 63
Gross Domestic Product, 97
Gross national product, 98
Guatemala, 60

Habib Bourguiba, 95
Haiti, 60
Hamilton, Bermuda, 94
Hans Morgenthau, 55
Harold E. Talbott, 78
Harold Hitz Burton, 81

Harold Macmillan, 44, 94, 105
Harold Stassen, 72
Harry S. Truman, 1, 2, 6, 23, 50, 74
Harvard Business School, 80
Hawaii, 47, 107
Hawaii Admission Act, 107
H-bomb, 46
Hellenic Parliament, 95
Help:Media, 33, 103
Help:Pronunciation respelling key, 5
Henri Giraud, 17
Henry B. Gonzalez, 51
Henry Cabot Lodge Jr., 74
Henry H. Arnold, 15, 56
Heo Jeong, 96
Herbert Brownell Jr., 30, 77, 78
Herbert Hoover, 5, 30, 49
Highway Trust Fund, 103
Historical rankings of Presidents of the United States, 113
History, 92
History of the United States Republican Party, 5
Hobo Day, 29
Ho Chi Minh, 88
Holocaust denial, 22
Holy See, 60
Honorary doctorate, 63
Hope, Kansas, 7
House Un-American Activities Committee, 99
Howard McCrum Snyder, 48
Hubert Humphrey, 96
Hungarian Peoples Republic, 40
Hungarian Revolution of 1956, 6, 40, 86
Hungary, 86

Ida Stover Eisenhower, 3, 7
IG Farben Building, 22
II Corps (United States), 17
I Like Ike, 28
Illegal immigration to the United States, 99
IMDb, 68
Immigrants to the United States, 99
Immigration and Nationality Act of 1952, 99
Immigration and Naturalization Service, 99
Imre Nagy, 86
India, 95
Infantry, 12
Inflation, 98
Intercontinental ballistic missile, 84
Intermediate-range ballistic missile, 92
International Atomic Energy Agency, 83
International Bible Students Association, 8
International Brotherhood of Teamsters, 106
International Geophysical Year, 105

International Standard Book Number, 64–67, 113–116
Internet Archive, 68
Interstate 290 (Illinois), 58
Interstate 70, 58
Interstate 80 in California, 58
Interstate Highway System, 4, 6, 33, 70, 72, 103
Interventionism (politics), 73
Invasion of Normandy, 5
Ira Chernus, 66
Iran, 95
Islamic Consultative Assembly (Iran), 95
Israeli–Palestinian conflict, 88
Italy, 94
Ivy League, 24
IX Corps (United States), 15

Jacobo Arbenz Guzmán, 85
James Buchanan, 29
James Campbell Hagerty, 79
James E. Chaney, 15
James Forrestal, 26
James P. Mitchell, 77, 79, 80
James R. Hoffa, 106
James T. Patterson (historian), 103, 114
Jawaharlal Nehru, 34, 48, 90, 95
JCS 1067, 23
Jean de Lattre de Tassigny, 25
Jean Edward Smith, 96, 114
Jehovahs Witness, 5
Jehovahs Witnesses, 8
Jimmy Carter, 56
Jim Thorpe, 9
J. Lawton Collins, 2, 42
John Diefenbaker, 94
John Eisenhower, 2, 10
John F. Kennedy, 1, 36, 43, 50, 54, 56, 71, 92
John Foster Dulles, 30, 76, 78, 120
John J. Pershing, 13
John Lewis Gaddis, 54, 113
John Marshall Harlan II, 47, 81
John Sparkman, 74
John W. Bricker, 85
John W. Goode, 51
John W. ODaniel, 42
Joint Chiefs of Staff, 23, 83
Jordan, 40, 90
Jorge Alessandri, 95
Joseph Dodge, 30, 78
Joseph Laniel, 94
Joseph L. Bristow, 9
Joseph McCarthy, 6, 29, 54, 81, 99
Joseph Stalin, 82
Joseph Swing, 99
Joseph T. McNarney, 2

Joseph W. Martin Jr., 46
J. Robert Oppenheimer, 46
JSTOR, 67
Julie Nixon Eisenhower, 10
Julius and Ethel Rosenberg, 100
Jury trial, 102
Juscelino Kubitschek, 95

Kabul, 95
Kansas, 5
Karachi, 95
Karlsbrunn, 6
Kenyon Joyce, 15
Kingdom of Greece (Glücksburg), 60
Kingdom of Yugoslavia, 61
Kingston upon Thames, 119
Konrad Adenauer, 94
Konstantinos Karamanlis, 95
Korea, 84
Korean War, 5, 72, 84, 93, 94
Ku Klux Klan, 101

Labor Management Relations Act of 1947, 106
Lancaster, Pennsylvania, 7
Landrum-Griffin Act, 106
Landslide election, 71
Lane University, 7
Laos, 43
Lavender Scare, 45
Leaders of South Vietnam, 42
Lebanon, 41
Lecompton, Kansas, 7
Legacy and memory, 4, 71
Legion of Honor, 60
Legion of Honor (Philippines), 61
Legion of Merit, 3, 59
Leonard T. Gerow, 15
Leonard W. Hall, 46
Lewis L. Strauss, 77
Library of Congress Control Number, 114
LibriVox, 68
Lieutenant colonel (United States), 12, 63, 64
Lieutenant general (United States), 64
Lisbon, 95
List of female United States Cabinet Secretaries, 78
List of Justices of the Supreme Court of the United States, 47
List of landmark court decisions in the United States, 101
List of memorials to Dwight D. Eisenhower, 4, 71
List of Presidents of Columbia University, 2
List of Presidents of the United States, 69, 71
List of Soviet Union–United States summits, 92
Little Rock, Arkansas, 102

Little Rock Central High School, 45, 54, 102
Little Rock Nine, 4, 6, 45, 71, 102
Lloyd Fredendall, 17
Lockheed U-2, 36, 37, 43, 92
London, 94
London and Paris Conferences, 86
Louisiana Maneuvers, 15
Louis St. Laurent, 94
Low Earth orbit, 105
Lucius D. Clay, 30, 78, 103
Lutheran, 5
Lyndon B. Johnson, 46, 52, 86
Lyndon Johnson, 55, 96

Madrid, 95
Mainland China, 88
Major general (United States), 16, 64
Major (United States), 12, 63
Mamie Eisenhower, 2, 5, 10
Manila, 95
Man In Space Soonest, 105
Manuel L. Quezon, 14
Manuel Quezon, 11
Mar del Plata, 95
Marginal, 98
Marion B. Folsom, 77
Marshall Plan, 25
Martin Luther King Jr., 45
Martin Patrick Durkin, 78
Martin P. Durkin, 77
Mary Jean Eisenhower, 10
Maryland, 12
Massive resistance, 101
Massive retaliation, 84
Matsu Islands, 39
Matthew Ridgway, 2, 42
Mayflower Hotel, 41
McCarthyism, 6, 54
McClellan Committee, 106
Médaille militaire, 60
Medal of Civic Merit, 61
Medal of Military Merit, 61
Mediterranean Theater of Operations, 15
Mennonite, 8
Mercury Seven, 106
Metropolitan Museum of Art, 121
Mexican Border Service Medal, 59
Mexico, 94, 96
Mexico–United States border, 99
MGM Records, 59
Midwestern United States, 72
Military career of Dwight D. Eisenhower, 3, 70
Military Demarcation Line, 38
Military–industrial complex, 50, 112
Military Governor of the U.S. Occupation Zone in Germany, 2

Military Medal (Luxembourg), 61
Military Order of Italy, 61
Military Order of the White Lion, 60
Miller Center of Public Affairs, 68
Milton Eisenhower, 14
Milton S. Eisenhower, 78
Missile gap, 4, 71, 92
Mohammad Mosaddegh, 40
Mohammad Reza Pahlavi, 39, 40, 95
Mohammed Mosaddeq, 85
Mohammed V of Morocco, 95
Mohammed Zahir Shah, 95
Money supply, 98
Montevideo, 95
Montreal, 94
Morocco, 61, 95
Mutual Defense Treaty Between the United States and the Republic of Korea, 84

Napalm, 42
NASA, 4, 6, 37, 71, 72, 105
Nassau-Saarbrücken, 6
National Aeronautics and Space Act, 6, 105
National Air and Space Museum, 59
National Army (USA), 63
National Assembly of South Korea, 96
National Association of Manufacturers, 78
National Congress of Brazil, 95
National Defense Education Act, 4, 6, 71, 106
National Defense Service Medal, 60
National Defense University, 58
National Governors Association, 73
National Guard of the United States, 102
National health insurance, 96
National Mall, 59
National memorial, 59
National Order of Honour and Merit, 60
National Park Service, 51
National security, 45, 72, 83
National Security Advisor (United States), 78
NATO, 73, 92
Navy Distinguished Service Medal, 59
Nazi concentration camps, 22
Nazi Germany, 100
Negative campaigning, 110
Neil H. McElroy, 77, 78
Nelson Rockefeller, 112
New Deal, 6, 31, 55, 72, 96
New Deal Coalition, 71
New Delhi, 95
New Hampshire primary, 74
New Look (policy), 4, 5, 35, 70, 83
News conference, 79
New York City, 26
New York Herald Tribune, 105
New York Republican State Committee, 72

Ngo Dinh Diem, 42, 88
Nikita Khrushchev, 35, 37, 44, 82, 87, 95
Nikolai Bulganin, 37, 94
Nishan-e-Pakistan, 61
Non-interventionism, 28, 72
Normandy landings, 3, 18, 19, 70
North Africa, 5
North Atlantic Council, 94
North Atlantic Treaty Organization, 26
North Korea, 84
North Vietnam, 42
Notable scholar surveys, 6
NSC 68, 85
Nuclear arms race, 54
Nuclear deterrence, 5
Nuclear power, 83
Nuclear proliferation, 92
Nuclear triad, 37, 83
Nuclear weapon, 72, 83
Nuclear weapons and the United States, 6
Nueva Ciudad Guerrero, 94
Nuremberg Trials, 23

Oak leaf cluster, 59
OCLC, 64–66, 115, 116
Office of Management and Budget, 78
Office of Military Government, United States, 22
Office of the Chief of Military History, 65
Oil painting, 11
Old Right (United States), 28
Omar Bradley, 2, 9, 56
On War, 13
Open Skies, 37
Operation Blue Bat, 41
Operation Dragoon, 19
Operation Overlord, 3, 18, 70
Operation Teapot, 39
Operation Torch, 5, 15
Operation Wetback, 99
Orden Vasco Núñez de Balboa, 61
Order of Abdon Calderón, 60
Order of Aeronautical Merit (Brazil), 60
Order of Glory (Tunisia), 61
Order of Ismail, 60
Order of Leopold (Belgium), 60
Order of Liberation, 60
Order of Manuel Amador Guerrero, 61
Order of Merit, 61
Order of Merit (Chile), 60
Order of Military Merit (Brazil), 60
Order of Ouissam Alaouite, 61
Order of Polonia Restituta, 61
Order of Sikatuna, 61
Order of Solomon, 60
Order of Suvorov, 61

Order of the Aztec Eagle, 61
Order of the Bath, 61
Order of the Chrysanthemum, 61
Order of the Cloud and Banner, 60
Order of the Elephant, 60, 62
Order of the Holy Sepulchre, 60
Order of the Liberator San Martin, 60
Order of the Netherlands Lion, 61
Order of the Oak Crown, 61
Order of the Queen of Sheba, 60
Order of the Redeemer, 60
Order of the Royal House of Chakri, 61
Order of the Southern Cross, 60
Order of Victory, 61, 62
Order of Virtuti Militari, 61
Order pro merito Melitensi, 61
Organized crime, 91
Orval Faubus, 45, 102
Oswald Jacoby, 11
Ottawa, 94
Oval Office, 50, 112
Oveta Culp Hobby, 30, 77, 78
Owens-Corning, 80

Pact of Madrid, 87
Pactomania, 41
Pakistan, 90, 92, 95
Palm Desert, California, 51
Panama, 61, 94
Panama Canal Zone, 13
Panama City, 94
Pan-Americanism, 90
Paris, 94
Parliament of India, 95
Partition of India, 90
Party divisions of United States Congresses, 96
Paul Douglas, 96
Paul Dudley White, 48
Paul of Greece, 95
Pennsylvania Dutch, 5, 7
Peoples Republic of China, 84
People to People International, 57
People to People Student Ambassadors, 57
PGM-17 Thor, 91
Pheochromocytoma, 49
Phi Beta Kappa, 24
Philippine Army, 14
Philippine Commonwealth, 14
Philippines, 95
Philip Sheridan, 56
Political machine, 112
Political party, 79
Pope John XXIII, 95
Portugal, 95
Potsdam Conference, 24, 92
Potter Stewart, 47, 81

Power vacuum, 89
Presbyterian Church (U.S.A.), 8
Presidency of Dwight D. Eisenhower, 4, 27, **69**, 70
Presidency of Harry S. Truman, 69, 73
Presidency of John F. Kennedy, 69
President of the Republic of China, 34
President of the United States, 1, 5, 17, 18, 69, 71, 76
Prime Minister of Egypt, 89
Prime Minister of India, 48
Prime Minister of Iran, 85
Prime Minister of the United Kingdom, 17, 105
Prisoner of war, 23
Procter & Gamble, 78
Project Genetrix, 37
Project Gutenberg, 68
Project Mercury, 106
Project Solarium, 35
Project Vanguard, 105
Public school (government funded), 101

Quemoy, 39
Quezon City, 14

Racial discrimination, 45
Racial segregation in the United States, 100
Radio Liberty, 86
Rajendra Prasad, 95
Ralph Flanders, 100
RDS-37, 35
Recess appointment, 81
Recession, 98
Recession of 1958, 6, 106
Reconstruction Era, 45, 76, 101
Red Army, 22
Refugee Relief Act, 99
Regular Army (United States), 63
Reichsautobahn, 33
Republican National Committee, 46
Republican Party presidential primaries, 1952, 4, 70, 72
Republican Party presidential primaries, 1956, 4, 70
Republican Party presidential primaries, 1960, 111
Republican Party (United States), 2, 27, 69, 71
Republic of China, 6, 39, 60, 88
Republic of China President, 87
Richard M. Nixon, 28
Richard Nixon, 1, 10, 41, 74, 76
Right-to-work law, 106
Rio de Janeiro, 95
River Brethren, 5, 8
Robert A. Taft, 5, 28, 45, 72
Robert B. Anderson, 32, 44, 77, 100

Robert Caro, 101
Robert Cutler, 78
Robert H. Jackson, 81
Robert Hugh Ferrell, 79
Robert Tripp Ross, 78
Rockefeller Republican, 72
Rock of Gibraltar, 15
Rollback, 82
Rome, 94
Royal Air Force, 92
Royal Norwegian Order of St. Olav, 61
Royal Order of George I, 60
Rudolf Abel, 44

Saint Lawrence Seaway, 104
Salerno landings, 17
Sam Rayburn, 46, 96
Samuel Eliot Morison, 77, 114
San Antonio, 15, 58
San Carlos de Bariloche, 95
Santiago, 95
São Paulo, 95
Saud of Saudi Arabia, 41
Scarlet fever, 10
Scholar survey results, 72
SEATO, 42
Seat of government, 69
Second inauguration of Dwight D. Eisenhower, 4, 70
Second Taiwan Strait Crisis, 88
Secretary of the Navy, 44
Security clearance, 79
Select or special committee (United States Congress), 106
Seoul, 93, 94
Sereno E. Brett, 13
Service star, 60
Sherman Adams, 48, 78
Sherman Minton, 81
Sicily, 5, 18
Simon & Schuster, 64
Sinai Peninsula, 89
Sinclair Weeks, 77, 78
Sino-American Mutual Defense Treaty, 88
Sino-Soviet split, 92
Six-Day War, 41
Sixth United States Army Group, 20
S:Korean Armistice Agreement, 84
Slate (magazine), 120
Small intestine, 48
Smith Act, 100
Smoky Hill River, 8
Social Security (United States), 6, 32, 72, 96
Social welfare, 72
South Dakota State University, 29
Southeast Asia, 88

Southeast Asia Treaty Organization, 88
Southern Germany, 22
Southern Manifesto, 101
South Korea, 84, 93, 94, 96
South Vietnam, 6, 42
Sovereign Military Order of Malta, 61
Sovereignty, 86
Soviet Empire, 73
Soviet Union, 5, 41, 43, 72, 73
Space Race, 6, 54
Spain, 87, 95
Spanish miracle, 87
S:Public Law 78-482, 56
Sputnik, 36
Sputnik 1, 105
Sputnik crisis, 4, 71
Sputnik I, 6
Standard Oil of New Jersey, 26
Stanley Forman Reed, 81
State legislature (United States), 107
State of the Union address, 44
State of Vietnam, 87
State visit, 42
St. Lawrence Seaway, 94
St. Marys University, Texas, 12
Strategic bomber, 84
Submarine-launched ballistic missile, 84
Suez Canal, 72, 89
Suez Crisis, 6, 40, 48, 72, 89
Supreme Allied Commander, 73
Supreme Allied Commander Europe, 1, 5
Supreme Commander of the Allied Expeditionary Force, 5
Supreme Court of the United States, 47, 81
Supreme Headquarters Allied Expeditionary Force, 3, 5, 15, 18, 70
Susan Eisenhower, 10
Switzerland, 94
Syngman Rhee, 38
Syria, 40, 90
Syrian Crisis of 1957, 6

Taipei, 87, 96
Taiwan, 87, 96
Taiwanese people, 87
Tank Corps, National Army, 12
Tank warfare, 13
Tau Epsilon Phi, 63
Tehran, 95
Template:Eisenhower series, 5, 71
Template talk:Eisenhower series, 5, 71
Tennessee Valley Authority, 96
Term limits in the United States, 72
Texas, 15, 99
Texas 20th congressional district, 51
Thailand, 61

The American Assembly, 25
The Church of Jesus Christ of Latter-day Saints, 78
The class the stars fell on, 9
The Metropolitan Museum of Art, 63
The New York Times, 68
Theodor Heuss, 94
The Pentagon, 23
The Royal Yugoslav Commemorative War Cross, 61
Thomas E. Dewey, 24, 72
Thomas E. Stephens, 11
Thomas S. Gates Jr., 77
Ticket (election), 73
Time (magazine), 109
Tin Lizzie, 11
Toll road, 103
Toulon, 95
Transcontinental Motor Convoy, 33
Treaty of San Francisco, 78
Tunisia, 61, 95
Tunisia Campaign, 17
Turkey, 95
Twelfth United States Army Group, 20
Twenty-second Amendment to the United States Constitution, 49, 72, 111
Twenty-third Amendment to the United States Constitution, 107

U-2 Crisis of 1960, 93
Ulysses S. Grant, 30
Union of Soviet Socialist Republics, 61
United Arab Republic, 90
United Fruit Company, 85
United Kingdom, 92, 94
United Nations Charter, 78
United States, 3, 63, 99, 123
United States Air Force, 91
United States Army, 3, 5, 10
United States Army Air Forces, 15
United States Army Central, 15
United States Army War College, 14
United States Atomic Energy Commission, 46
United States Attorney General, 77
United States Border Patrol, 99
United States Capitol, 53
United States Capitol rotunda, 59
United States Commission on Civil Rights, 101
United States Congress, 59
United States Constitution, 107
United States Courts of Appeals, 81
United States Department of Health, Education, and Welfare, 32, 78
United States Department of Justice, 45
United States Department of Justice Civil Rights Division, 102

United States district courts, 81
United States elections, 1958, 107
United States embargo against Cuba, 91
United States Military Academy, 3, 5, 63
United States National Security Council, 78, 83
United States Naval Academy, 8
United States Postmaster General, 77
United States presidential election, 1952, 4, 5, 28, 70, 71
United States presidential election, 1956, 4, 32, 70, 71, 109
United States presidential election, 1960, 71, 111
United States presidential inauguration, 71
United States Secretary of Agriculture, 77
United States Secretary of Commerce, 77
United States Secretary of Defense, 77
United States Secretary of Health, Education, and Welfare, 77
United States Secretary of Labor, 77
United States Secretary of State, 76
United States Secretary of the Air Force, 78
United States Secretary of the Interior, 77
United States Secretary of the Treasury, 77
United States Secret Service, 50
United States Senate elections, 1954, 46
Up or out, 56
Uprising of 1953 in East Germany, 86
Uruguay, 95
U.S. Department of the Treasury, 25
U.S. Navy, 44
U.S. Secretary of Defense, 26
U.S. state, 75, 107

Vanguard TV3, 105
Vatican City, 95
Veterans Day (United States), 55
Vice President of the United States, 1, 76
Vichy France, 17
Victory in Europe Day, 3, 70
Việt Minh, 87
Vietnam, 88
Vincent Massey, 94
Virtuti Militari, 24

Walter Krueger, 15
Walter Reed Army Medical Center, 53
War Cross (Belgium), 60
Warren Court, 80
Warsaw Pact, 72, 86
Washington, D.C., 2, 69, 99
Washington National Cathedral, 53
W. Averell Harriman, 110
Wendell Willkie, 72
Wendy Beckett, 11
Wernher von Braun, 37

Western bloc, 82
Western Desert Campaign, 17
Western European Union, 86
Western Front (World War II), 5, 19
West Germany, 82, 94
West Point, 10
Whistle stop train tour, 75
White House, 11, 49, 69
White House Chief of Staff, 55, 78
White House Press Secretary, 79
Wikipedia:Citation needed, 8, 12, 110
Wikipedia:Verifiability, 15
Wikt:wishy-washy, 78
William B. Pickett, 66, 115
William Howard Taft, 30
William J. Brennan, 47, 81
William Knowland, 45, 107
William McChesney Martin, 80
William P. Rogers, 77
Winston Churchill, 14, 17, 21, 82
World Golf Hall of Fame, 63
World War I, 3, 5, 12
World War II, 3, 5, 15
World War II Victory Medal, 60
World War II Victory Medal (United States), 3
World War I Victory Medal (United States), 3, 60
WP:NOTRS, 53

Yalta Agreement, 46
York, Pennsylvania, 6

Zachary Taylor, 30
Zane Grey, 11

www.ingramcontent.com/pod-product-compliance
Lightning Source LLC
Chambersburg PA
CBHW031947070426
42453CB00007BA/405